THE WIND RUNNER

THE WINE RUNNER

My Year of Hard Yards and Vineyards

COLIN RENTON

POLARIS
PUBLISHING

This edition first published in 2023 by

POLARIS PUBLISHING LTD
c/o Aberdein Considine
2nd Floor, Elder House
Multrees Walk
Edinburgh
EH1 3DX

www.polarispublishing.com

Text copyright © Colin Renton, 2023

ISBN: 9781915359056
eBook ISBN: 9781915359063

British Library Cataloguing-in-Publication Data
A catalogue record for this book is available on request from the British Library.

Designed and typeset by Polaris Publishing, Edinburgh
Printed in Great Britain by MBM Print, East Kilbride

In memory of Dad,
who introduced me to the joys of running.

CONTENTS

Acknowledgements

The plan had been brewing for some time when I first mentioned it to those whose help would be essential to make it happen. Once I had established the framework, my focus turned to identifying the people I would rely on. There were many. Without their support, encouragement and reassurance, this book would never have materialised.

My father's influence made me a runner. That was many years ago. When it came to this project, he took a great interest in my progress. My marathon in Austria was on his birthday. When I called him later in the day, he was typically enthusiastic about my achievement and keen to know more. I am saddened that he did not live to see this book's publication. I dedicate it to him.

It was a pleasure to work with Pete at Polaris Publishing. He provided supportive feedback at every stage. His guidance and encouragement steered me seamlessly through the publication process.

My editor, Martin, cast his experienced eye over my work and offered helpful suggestions, including an amendment to the title. It was reassuring to have the backing and direction of a seasoned professional.

I met some fabulous people on my travels. The passion of volunteers involved in race organisation, stewarding and other unseen tasks is impressive. Without them, running, and sport in general, would be a poorer place. That is particularly true of parkruns, where those involved do the job with great humour and commitment on a weekly basis.

Passion was also an overriding characteristic when it came to identifying the people who would educate me about wine. I was fortunate with my choices, which meant I was in the hands of individuals who were happy to share their knowledge in an entertaining way. Athos in Italy, Morna in England and Gábor in Hungary imparted their expertise with great wit and patience. I also had the privilege of learning about the personal commitment to winemaking from Francisco in Portugal and Frédéric in France, as well as the delightful and tireless Jeanette in Belgium.

One of the features of the book is the music I listened to as I ran. It was a voyage of rediscovery which revived tunes from my past, some that were inspirational and others that induced nostalgia and comfort during training. The soundtrack was the work of my daughter, Ellen. She may not agree with the sounds of my youth, but she clearly knows her dad given her appropriate choices.

Although it was largely a solo project, I had company for three of my trips. My friend Mike was with me in Belgium. He adapted effortlessly to my habit of wandering, sometimes aimlessly, in order to learn about new destinations. My time in Dinant was enjoyable, and that was largely due to him being there.

My son, Lewis, was great fun, as always, when he took time out of his hectic timetable – including preparations for his wedding and an ironman triathlon – to join me in Andalucia. Father/son time is always special, but in this case his linguistic skills, knowledge of Spain, and his encouragement as I struggled during the run, made it a particular pleasure.

And completing the family input was my wife, Caroline, who provided unwavering reassurance throughout the adventure. She joined me in Portugal, which was one of my toughest races. She never questioned my plan, although she probably had her doubts at times. I am grateful to her for that resolute support and encouragement.

Introduction

WARM-UP

I fire the starting pistol for this adventure during the first Covid lockdown of 2020. Sometimes, it's dangerous when you have time to think.

Like others around the world, I'm confined to the house with my family. I'm reading about the baking, the language learning, the home tutoring of children and the many other activities that are occupying the time that people would ordinarily use for work, travel and socialising.

Meanwhile, I'm making plans. They revolve around my passions for running, travelling, writing and wine. The idea that I might be able to combine all four in a single project is gathering momentum, fuelled by an imminent departure from my job as a corporate writer and entry into semi-retirement. It gradually evolves into a schedule for a non-negotiable, once-in-a-lifetime endeavour.

Running: There's the desire to don my kit for races in appealing European locations. The overriding objective is that stubbornly unfulfilled ambition of completing a marathon. It has teased me for many years, but the closest I have come was half the classic distance. That was almost four decades ago.

Travelling: I will take pleasure from weighing up my options, choosing my destinations and from the background reading that will educate me on local history, customs and the landscape the runs will cover. I'm familiar with some of the places on my prospective list, but others will be a journey into the unknown.

Writing: There's the book I haven't yet written. False starts aplenty have littered my writing career. The two unfinished novels plus two non-fiction works that didn't make it past the opening chapters are evidence of the more pressing deadlines that took precedence.

Wine: I have a box where, alongside my education certificates and confirmation of professional qualifications, lurks a document declaring that I 'satisfied the examiners' that I knew a little about the subject back in 1996. Now, the looming desk-free days present a chance to use my travels as an excuse to sip and slurp my way to greater knowledge.

Each of the trips will feature a race and a tasting – either a formal arrangement or a self-conducted sampling. I might visit producers or track down specialist bars. In some cases, I may even combine running with tasting during a race.

My research will conclude with me choosing one wine that is either typical of the area or represents my experience of that trip, the idea being to create a mixed case of twelve bottles to summarise my running year. When making my selection, I don't want to focus solely on the wine tasting aspect. There are many people better qualified than I am to talk about varietals, bouquets, fermentation or tannins. I want to learn more about the places, the people, and the stories behind the winemaking process.

Before the pandemic, I was a regular gym goer. The UK lockdown has led me to abandon the treadmill, cross-trainer and static bike for the paths and parks of Scotland's capital city and a rediscovery of the joys of running.

The notion that I was reasonably fit for a man galloping towards the end of his sixth decade has been swiftly erased. The reality of running on roads rather than zipping along on a machine, unencumbered by underfoot undulations or variable weather conditions, has proved to be more challenging than I had expected.

Little by little, I graduate from puffing my way along a pancake flat mile in a time best measured by a sundial rather than a stopwatch. Slowly – obviously – and steadily, I add distance and eventually manage to move my ageing limbs at a slightly quicker pace, deriving great satisfaction from my ability to eke out another mile or two as the weeks slip by, in the process building belief that I will be able to achieve the planned race distances.

I consider music to be an essential training partner, so it is not only me that shuffles as I run – the sounds of an earlier life also flick from track to track and provide the accompaniment. I haven't listened to many tunes over recent years, and the playlist my daughter Ellen has kindly compiled for her technophobe dad reflects her knowledge of my tastes and age, featuring artists who brought colour to my youth – welcome back Electric Light Orchestra, Supertramp and Dire Straits. As a bit of fun, I will choose one of the songs from my playlist, or perhaps find something else relevant to the occasion, as tune of the day when it comes to documenting each of my races.

Now, with my fitness on a gentle upward trajectory, I start to think about the nuances of my plan. Most races take place early in the day, a fact that is largely incompatible with my sluggishness in the morning. I need to adjust my body clock. I gently nudge forward my runs from the evening to a time that ensures I will be good to go, whether it is dawn, dusk, or any stage in between, then I complete some Saturday morning events to test that theory.

Progress in training is often laborious and I'm frequently reminded that running a marathon is a considerable physical challenge. It can take days to shrug off even a minor twinge, and confidence vies with doubt for mental supremacy as the need to prove that this was more than a romantic notion edges closer.

I turn my attention to the schedule. Inserting 'Wine Run' into a search engine elicits a surprising number of results. Narrowing it down to just twelve is no simple process. Diversity of countries, range of distances, and degrees of difficulty merely emphasise the size of this athletic universe and complicate the task of choosing which races will feature.

Leaving work halfway through 2021 allows me a few months to plot my travel itinerary, register for races – something that occasionally proves more problematic than I had imagined – and, minor detail, get myself fit enough to take on the challenges presented by different terrains, variable conditions and distances ranging from five kilometres to twenty-six miles. There will be thigh-burning climbs, dusty paths through scenic landscape, energy-sapping muddy fields and mile after mile of tarmac in countries around Europe.

Ultimately, I opt for a spread that exposes me to an intriguing variety of courses, people, and cultures. I can contemplate visits to places such as Switzerland, Slovenia and Belgium, which are not – to me at least – particularly renowned wine producing countries. Among my other possible destinations are some with greater traditions, including France, Italy and Spain.

Despite the assortment, all can be categorised in some way as wine runs. It's a generic label that describes many events around Europe and beyond, with the emphasis in some cases on the run, while others give greater weight to the wine aspect.

Although it's a combination that may not earn rave reviews from modern nutritional experts – particularly in the cases where alcohol is dispensed during races – running and wine have a long association. The origins are widely believed to date back to the early nineteenth century when vineyard proprietors in France encouraged their workers to improve fitness levels ahead of the physically demanding annual grape harvest. At that time, wine was regarded as a performance-enhancing substance.

In the modern era, running through vines has many attractions. The terrain is varied, traffic-free, frequently testing in its contours, and often idyllic. There is limited disruption to the daily lives of locals, runners have a chance to enjoy the freedom of open spaces and the company of other like-minded individuals, while a festive spirit is invariably the order of the day.

Serious runners can win substantial prizes and major kudos. Those with less talent can enjoy the social aspect of running, the chance to shave a few seconds off their personal best time, or the simple satisfaction of reaching the finish. Many, it seems, relish the opportunity to participate in a fancy dress parade of sorts, often wearing costumes that exhibit much imagination and effort.

Producers have an opportunity to promote their wines to a wider audience, whether that is through awarding an amount equal to the winners' weight, handing out a bottle to all finishers, supplying wines at refreshment stops, or just by allowing race routes to pass through their vines.

While many of the dates on my schedule are formal wine runs, I round out the month-by-month racing programme with a few that have no official link but where I can stitch together my own running/tasting combination. The parameters I have applied mean I am forced to make some difficult choices. The result is a wine run calendar that some may find fault with, but which presents me with the range of challenges I am seeking.

I know there will be no podium finishes, nor will I become a Master of Wine, but I want to improve my performances and knowledge on both fronts.

I am conscious that the planned travel will land me with a sizeable carbon footprint, so I commit to looking at ways to offset or, at the very least, limit my impact. Using public transport could help in that regard and will also introduce me to real life in the countries I plan to visit – off-the-beaten-track villages served by irregular bus services, and an unvarnished view of how people go about their daily lives obscured from the tourist's eye that has previously coloured my impressions.

I will favour hotels with strong ethics or links to charitable causes and focus on supporting businesses with a principled outlook, while reassessing some of my own lifestyle and habits. I will also try to track down winemakers who endeavour to operate ethically.

Initially, my plan was to start my schedule in January, a month after my sixtieth birthday. However, events surrounding Covid have been a timely reminder of the need to seize the day. I am healthy and relatively fit, while my initial planning has gone fairly well.

It makes sense to finish with the biggest challenge, a marathon, which I have pencilled in for September 2022. With that as the ultimate target, I decide to make a start in October, rather than kick my heels for another three months.

One

SWITZERLAND

TUNE OF THE DAY:
'Running Up That Hill' — Kate Bush

*H*e's yodelling. The high-viz-jacketed workman is yodelling as he waits for the cement mixer to spew forth its contents. My aim is to challenge Swiss clichés, and this is not a good start. I've travelled here believing there is more to Switzerland than adeptness at making cuckoo clocks and multi-purpose knives or providing discreet banking services for the wealthy. And I'm confident its people don't deserve their reputation for being a little dull, or for their ability to yodel. Perhaps I was wrong.

Today they will have a chance to scotch the myth about their humdrum personalities as they dispense food and drink, and bonhomie. For my part, I will launch my year-long twelve-stage challenge by covering twenty-one-and-a-half kilometres through the Chemin du Vignoble, the vineyard trail around Sion. Despite covering only half the full distance, this event is called the Marathon des Saveurs.

Organisers pitch it as suitable for those who are sporty gourmets or gourmet sportspeople, and the official website suggests that a hearty appetite is as essential as a reasonable level of fitness.

Picturesque Sion is still mostly asleep as I join other runners on their way to the starting point and we mingle with the odd resident out for an early morning stroll. It's a quaint and scrupulously clean town of around 30,000 people that punches above its weight in terms of culture, and is the capital of the Valais, one of Switzerland's twenty-six cantons, or states.

Four languages are spoken by different population groups across the country – German, Italian and Romansh (whose users are declining in number) as well as French, which is the dominant tongue in this region.

Most days, the town centre is abuzz with drinkers and diners sitting at tables outside cafés, bars and restaurants in the Place du Midi and the boutique-lined Rue de la Porte-Neuve. The town is the canton's administrative centre and the local government headquarters overlook the Place de la Planta, which also boasts a tourist office, café, children's play area and a statue of Helvetia, the female personification of the Swiss Confederation. An information board at the entrance to the square explains that the Battle of la Planta took place in 1475, during the Burgundy wars.

Today the space is dominated by an inflatable arch, which marks the starting line for the event and boasts that 'Valais is engraved in my heart' in French and in German. There are also tables where participants collect the essentials for the challenge ahead – a train ticket for the return trip, a water bladder, a commemorative glass, which is set to be well used, and a book of vouchers, which will be exchanged for food and wine at each of the feeding stations.

It's chilly now, but the forecast is good and, to the relief of those who have been here before and understand the vagaries of conditions locally, no rain is expected. The announcer may have been introduced as Eric, although I didn't hear it clearly. He reminds us in both of the common languages that this is definitely not a race. Runners are urged not to go too quickly as to do so might spoil the enjoyment of a breathtaking landscape that rises 850 metres as it traverses the peaks and valleys on mixed terrain. I'm happy to take things calmly, particularly as a stubborn calf injury has hampered my preparations. My plan is to drink in the stunning views as well as the wines served at each of the five stops. Nevertheless, I've seen some of the terrain and, given that altitude gain, I'm expecting to be tested physically.

I have signed up for a route that heads west towards the Chamoson municipality – the most densely planted part of the Valais vineyard – and concludes in the town of St-Pierre-de-Clages, which is renowned for its antiquarian bookshops as well as its fifty or so wine cellars. Dubbed 'the Conquest of the West', this option is new and is in addition to the traditional one, launched in 2019 and traversing the irrigation channels or *bisses* that run from Sion in an easterly direction. As well as allowing more participants overall, offering a choice means regulars can have a change of scenery and a chance to sample different local wines. Maybe it's an excuse for me to come back at some point in the future and tick that other box by doing the original version.

For now, I have plenty to focus on. Although it is not compulsory, I see this as a running challenge and I want to push myself if I can in order to assess my fitness. By contrast, many participants are here for a gentle day out rather than a physical test. Of the 1,000 or so entrants, a good number are dressed for hiking.

Small groups start twenty minutes apart in order to prevent congestion around the course, and there is a jovial mood among those waiting to be sent on their way as part of the latest wave. A dozen or so are repelling the cold with a group ritual that is followed by a shot of something alcoholic that has them raring to go as they prepare to set off in an easterly direction.

Eric appears to fit the Swiss stereotype. Despite the baseball cap and hoodie, he looks like someone who spends Monday to Friday doing an important but unexciting desk job; the type of guy who would be reluctant go on stage at a karaoke night but would then be impossible to budge. He's now in full flow, switching with ease from French to German and doing a fine job, but everyone is ready to move and there is an element of relief when he finishes talking.

We exit the square and head for the relatively car-free streets out of Sion. I decide to try and warm up my shivering muscles with an easy jog, and by the time I have spied the next red sign that indicates the direction we should be following, I'm clear of the others who started with me. Many have set off at a pace that suggests the only thing dictating the extent of their effort will be the need to arrive at the finish before the course closes at 6pm.

I lengthen my stride as I head out of town and encounter a pedestrian who doesn't appear to have complete control of the dogs she is putatively in charge of. I steer clear and continue on my way. A few minutes later I reach a roundabout with numerous exits and no red signs. I decide that I have missed a turn and should head back.

I retrace my steps and, as suspected, my focus on the errant dogs has caused me to pass a sign. Back on track, a steep climb allows me to go past some stragglers and reconnect with the others before settling into a rhythm. We've been going for a couple of miles when we hit a narrow lakeside path that rules out any overtaking.

As we pass the Lake of Montorge, effort is needed to avoid the puddles. But despite the dampness underfoot, the sun is breaking through and temperatures are already on the rise. A couple of Londoners are contrasting the favourable conditions with the rain that dampened their spirits the last time they were here. The lake is renowned for its wildlife and plants, and those with a little more time to do touristy things can increase their knowledge with a visit to the Maison de la Nature, which sits on its banks.

We emerge from the forest and, as I reaccustom my legs to the hard road, we negotiate a bend and confront a babble of noise. This is the Montorge winery. Upended barrels provide makeshift tables and the group that started twenty minutes ahead are enjoying their first halt of the day. Some sit at the roadside to catch a few rays of sunshine and enjoy a dish of cheeses and charcuterie. This offering is labelled apéro, while the next four stops will represent a starter, two main dishes and a dessert.

As that group polishes off the food and the two accompanying wines before resuming, I exchange the first of the vouchers in my booklet for the dish and use the plate to reserve an available barrel. It does feel a little early in the day to be drinking wine. I debate this fact for a few seconds before unhitching my glass from my light backpack and succumbing to the lure of a Fendant Grand Cru from the Dubuis & Rudaz winery in Sion. It is light and refreshing, with the merest hint of gas, and is an excellent start to my day.

Fendant is the most widely known wine from the Valais. The name can only appear on the label of bottles made from the Chasselas grape. Fendant, I learn, is derived from fendre, the French word that means split and is apposite in this case because the ripe grapes burst open to the touch rather than needing to be squeezed to release their juice.

I'm joined at my barrel by a Swiss couple and, while he is collecting supplies, she tells me that she has taken part each year since 2019, including the 2020 edition when Covid replaced the rain as the big mood dampener. I sense a hint of disdain when I ask whether they live in Sion, and she pointedly tells me they are from Bern.

It's then her turn to get the second wine in and she heads off to the bar for two glasses of Dôle Hurlevent, a red made by the sons of Charles Favre, owners of the Montorge winery. Dôle is a name used exclusively in the Valais region and is a blend of Pinot Noir and Gamay, traditional grapes that are grown in large volume nearby and come together to create a distinctively Swiss style.

The husband tells me in German that he speaks no English. Perhaps that's a hint that he doesn't want to engage. Instead, I search in the deepest recesses of my memory for the linguistic tools honed in my schooldays and unused since I spent a weekend in Berlin over a decade ago. He tells me they drove down in order to stock up on wine and enjoy the hike. They are athletes who have completed marathons, and they admit that they expected a greater running element when they registered for the inaugural event. However, it has not deterred them from becoming regulars. They have clearly been training hard in the wine-tasting aspect as, having arrived behind me, they are ready to resume before I have taken a drop of my red, and with a cheery 'viel spass', they urge me to enjoy the experience then they disappear into the distance.

Another couple take a place at the next barrel. They cast critical eyes over everyone and offer detailed analysis. I become the topic of their chat and, in a stage whisper, she announces, 'No, no, he left at the same time as us.'

I'm not sure what the conversation is about, but I do know it's time to get going. I can see that the temptation to linger will increase as the day progresses but, although it is not strictly regulated, organisers are keen that there should be a maximum halt of thirty minutes to prevent congestion at each of the stops, and I have no plans to spend that long.

Despite the shock to my digestive system – it's not yet 10 o'clock – I soon recover a slow, comfortable running pace and I overtake a group that includes my new Swiss friends. Then we are forced to walk in single file through a vineyard, and almost come a cropper on the sheer descent of a pebbled path. Many of the spaces between the vines are man-made gravel tracks, as that surface helps to retain the heat that boosts the growth of the grapes, although it's not always ideal for running.

The sun is starting to make its presence felt as we reach a main road, where a concerned member of the organisational team is waiting to ensure we avoid being mown down as we cross. That's unlikely given the almost total absence of traffic, although a grape-laden tractor does trundle by, presumably driven by a farmer who has begun to harvest some of his crop.

The space opens out and I am weighing up another opportunity to raise the pace a little when the sound of more raised voices and boisterous laughter signals stop number two. A cheery man ladles butternut squash soup into a bowl and insists we take bread – gluten-free if we wish – before I find space at a table. This is Tour Lombarde, a modern space with a substantial tasting room as well as an exhibition area and a large facility that hosts business meetings. Vouchers change hands and I come back to the table with my glass replenished. The white is a Chardonnay from Cave du Tunnel. The grape was brought to this part of the world from France in the 1920s and, although a little lighter than its French relative, there is a nod to Burgundy in the rich, buttery flavours. That is followed by the red, a Pinot Noir from Cave la Tine, poured by a gnarly man with a cheery disposition and the reddened face of someone who works outside in all weathers. His wine is light and fruity, and quickly gone.

A tinkling water fountain is used to wash out wineglasses and top up the bladder that was part of our welcome pack. And then it is back into action. I typically wouldn't run within two hours of eating, so I had assumed today would be a test for my constitution. I feel remarkably good and the soup does not weigh too heavily as I enjoy the freedom to jog a little before catching some of those ahead of me as we climb up several stone steps into vines that are laden with grapes.

Again, my pace of consumption at the feeding stations seems to be lacking, as I pass a man I had overtaken shortly before the most recent stop.

The groups may have set off at twenty-minute intervals, but they are now amorphous and scattered throughout the vines. We come down off the hill and pass through a village where another vigneron is offering the opportunity to test his wines. He is not part of the official programme and it's unclear whether he has set up in opposition or is piggy-backing on the official tastings to showcase his produce. I resist his proposition and continue on my way. This long flat expanse is part of an official walking trail, so it's a little more benign than some of the earlier sections. That gives me another chance to accelerate a little.

I have always understood that the task of planting, growing and harvesting grapes is huge. Only when I see the acres of uneven land and the number of plants in each plot do I fully appreciate what being a winegrower in this region entails. And that's before the maker's skill comes into the picture in creating the final product. The extent of the effort is emphasised even further when I glance to my right and see the steepness of the hill. No equipment could possibly operate in some of these spaces. So, while there's little doubt that a good year will be lucrative, it's equally clear that the economic benefits are hard-earned.

The Valais produces around half of all Swiss wine, making the industry the platform on which the regional economy is built. The importance of winemaking to this part of Switzerland was clear as the train on which I travelled from Geneva whizzed through row after flawless row of painstakingly planted vines that sit on the edge of the track and extend high into the hills that loom above. Water – and its ability to regulate the heat – plays a crucial role in the success of grape-growing and the fast-flowing Rhône, which passes through Sion on the early part of its journey to the Mediterranean, is key to the Valais. The river is an integral tool for the town's wine industry, with most of the vineyards situated on the right bank, meaning they benefit from the sun.

Vines are packed into neat lines as far as the eye can see. It looks like the work of a draughtsman, or a Cézanne landscape that captures all of the aching beauty of the countryside, and combines it with the brutal harshness of the relentless work that is hidden from view.

It's a spectacular sight, each patch of grapes seemingly planted to symmetrical perfection and now offering the appearance of an immaculate commune between humans and nature. The current peacefulness is at odds with the full extent of the harvest that will come shortly, when the vineyards become a hive of activity and the race against the elements is won or lost.

The lifestyle may seem idyllic, but I'm conscious that its tenuous nature is ever present. Adverse climatic conditions – too much frost, too much rain, and too much sunshine at the wrong time of year – can destroy the fruit. I have also read tales in the local newspaper, *Le Nouvelliste*, about other problematic issues, with some high-profile winemakers reporting the theft of grapes on such a scale that it is clearly the work of gangs prepared to spend several hours picking the fruit and transporting it to where it might be sold. The nocturnal activities are particularly frustrating for the growers, as many of the grapes are not yet fully ripe. The result is that police have stepped up the frequency of their checks and the winemakers are adopting more security measures to protect their precious crops.

The sun is now high in the sky and the familiar cackle of a crowd rises from a car park at the foot of the hill I am descending. This is the Salle de la Pontaise, a community building for the Ardon area. Today, it has been transformed into an outdoor dining space. Several groups have come together and there is a queue for the raclette that is being served. This is traditional peasant food from the Valais but has moved upmarket in recent years. It has now found its way onto menus in many plush restaurants around the world and is a favourite après-ski dish.

The chef is working at an impressive rate, dishing it up with the traditional accompaniments of small potatoes, cornichons and pickled onions. The number of people waiting grows as a potato shortage strikes. One of his team distributes apple juice to quench thirsts and fill the time until the problem is resolved and the raclette can be served to the throng. To create it, the chef uses a specialist grill to melt the flat side of a round cheese that has been cut in half, then scrapes the resulting gooey deliciousness onto a plate.

The wine is something of a revelation. It's a Païen d'Ardon from the Cave la Madeleine, fruity, light and a delicious companion for the raclette. It is made from grapes known elsewhere as Savagnin Blanc or Traminer and this is the first wine I've come across today involving women makers – the daughters of André Fontannaz are involved in the process, underlining that this traditionally male-dominated business is slowly modernising. The red, an aromatic and spicy Gamay from the Cave Rives du Bisse, is an equally alluring partner to the dish. Great food, lovely wine and a seat on a courtyard bench in the sun all add up to a fun way to spend a Saturday afternoon, but there is still some distance to cover, so I haul myself to my feet and get going.

Once more I'm surprisingly comfortable as I resume at a jog. This time the way ahead is relatively clear and I catch a couple who are tempted by the grapes. They confirm that the handful they have tasted were indeed delicious. A climb so steep that running is ruled out is followed by a section along the narrow concrete blocks that separate the vines. These walls are the only way to create the terraces that allow the plants to grow in such precipitous terrain while maximising the productiveness of the available space, as well as boosting irrigation. Below me is a sheer drop and I question whether Swiss health & safety know what's going on today. There are very few participants around and I have just passed the only people I have seen for some time when I hear a whistle. It seems I have overshot another turning and one of them is pointing out my error.

I get back on track then, as I pick my way through a heavily wooded area, I wonder how easy it might be to locate a missing individual should they wander astray. As I'm considering whether I may be that person, I see a red sign and the path kicks sharply upwards, allowing me to enjoy the solitude as well as the physical effort. Twigs crack underfoot and leaves rustle as I continue solo before light breaks through the trees, I cross a bridge and before me is the next stop, the Restaurant La Préfecture.

No one else is here apart from the staff. I'm invited to take a seat and a waitress delivers mushroom en croûte, a flavour-packed dish with a pastry surround that is lighter than it appears and as tasty as everything that has gone before.

I hand over the relevant voucher then also swap one for a chilled glass of Johannisberg from Cave Petite Vertu, served by Patrick Schmaltzried, a vineyard owner and salesman who is here in person, pitching an excellent white wine that is made in a neighbouring village by his son. I don't suppose he will see many sales, despite the deliciously sweet and fruity product, which features the region's second-most popular grape variety – Johannisberg is known elsewhere as Silvaner and benefits particularly from the geography of this part of the Valais. A glass of Cornalin red, produced a wine cork's throw from here at the renowned Maurice Gay estate, which has been around since 1883, sets me up for the final haul to the finishing line, which I know is only a couple of miles away.

Before I leave, two couples arrive and occupy the neighbouring table. One of the men wants to wish me 'santé' and we clink glasses. I realise they may be here some time, as will the group of people who order beers as they enter.

It's now downhill, perhaps figuratively as well as geographically, and I have an opportunity to jog to the finish in Saint-Pierre-de-Clages, passing farms, houses and eventually shops. If I was going to sketch a Swiss landscape with all its typical attributes, it would look like the descent into Saint-Pierre-de-Clages. Snow-peaked mountains fill the horizon and vines sprawl around a quaint village. This is the Switzerland that inhabits my imagination.

I cross the finishing line and, once inside the welcome tent, I'm tended to by a group of enthusiastic volunteers who serve up a Johannisberg tart – a delicacy around here. It is made with ingredients that include crème fraîche and, of course, wine, together with two more matched drinks. The first is a white produced by René Favre and sons from another indigenous grape, the Petite Arvine, which can be traced back to the seventeenth century, and is ideal with desserts. Then my adventure ends with a red from another family winery – Daniel Magliocco and son. It is a mix of Cornalin and Humagne Rouge grapes that is fruity and light and is a pleasurable finish to my day of tasting. The experience has been enjoyable and testing, and different in many respects to what I expected. It's certainly the first time I've drunk more than the maximum daily recommended units of alcohol while I've been out running.

It has taken me almost three hours to cover roughly the half-marathon distance, with enforced slowing at narrow passages and steep sections among the vines hindering my progress, while the various stops have added significantly to that time.

Others arrive and the space fills up, so I decide to leave them to it. I check out the deserted streets and look in the windows of nearby second-hand bookshops. I had hoped that I might meet Jamie McCulloch to learn a little more about what prompted a Scot to choose Switzerland as the place to pursue, with a significant amount of success, his winemaking ambitions. Unfortunately, Jamie is not around this weekend. He is back home in Scotland. Nevertheless, my curiosity is aroused and I decide to seek out his place, which I know is close. It means climbing back up the final hill for a short distance. I'm halfway up when I hear jovial cheering. It's my mate from the previous stop wishing me 'santé' once more.

I also bump into a couple that I saw earlier and, with his tongue planted firmly in his cheek, he asks whether I'm now doing the course in reverse. I confirm that that's not my intention, then, having identified the place where Jamie McCulloch weaves his magic to create some acclaimed wines, I walk back downhill to the railway station where clusters of people wait for the train back to Sion.

In their hands they clutch the rail tickets they were handed earlier. To my surprise, one has succumbed to the sales pitch at stop number four, because he is holding a box containing three bottles of Johannisberg – a result for Patrick Schmaltzried.

We are joined on the train by a boisterous stag party, dressed in Hawaiian gear and with the groom in ladies clothing. They provide harmless entertainment on the short trip, causing hilarity among the other passengers and at least partially dismissing the theory about the Swiss being dull.

It's now time to reflect a little on what I've learned. Around ninety-eight per cent of Swiss wine is destined for the domestic market, so it's easy to understand why so little is known outside the country about the variety of styles and quality. Over the day, I experienced some of that variety. Now I'm looking to find out a bit more about Valais wines and particularly those from Sion.

The best way to improve my knowledge is by spending the next day strolling. Sion draws on a history dating back 7,000 years and now labels itself 'Capitale des Vins' in recognition of the high quality – and high volume – of wines made in and around the town. As I meander through the cobbled streets, I notice that this place is a great fit for pun-rich business names. There's an eye specialist called Opti-Sion and a restaurant named La Fabrik' à Sion, where the fabrication is limited to dishes created from local ingredients.

However, it's clear that, unlike Fridays when the town is buzzing with activity and the market is in full swing, Sundays are a day of rest. Few people have left their homes, while shops and many of the cafés and bars remain closed. I guess that Eric will be reflecting on his moment in the sun yesterday morning and contemplating being back at his desk tomorrow.

The residents I do encounter are walking, some dressed for an energetic hike, others for a less vigorous outing. Those in the first group strike out for the same peaks that I experienced, while the not so active prefer to meet friends in the town centre.

Evidence of the thriving economy in the town is the ongoing construction activity and the modernity of the Energypolis Campus, where students and researchers work on the technology that will define the future role of health and energy for various industries.

The contrast of such a cutting-edge establishment with the town's ancient monuments is stark. I wander up to the Castle of Valère. Built using a combination of Romanesque and Gothic styles, it has held its dominant position high above Sion since the eleventh century. It was home to canons of the cathedral chapter of Sion until the late eighteenth century. Today it's the location of the Valais History Museum and home to what is believed to be one of the world's oldest functioning organs, understood to have been built in 1435. During a visit in 1984, Pope John Paul II categorised the church as a minor basilica.

Sitting at an even higher attitude on a hill that faces Valère, and reached using a path that is at times steep and narrow, the Castle of Tourbillon was built by Bishop Boniface 200 years later. In the thirteenth century, this was the summer residence of the bishops of Sion. It was ravaged by fire in 1788 and is now a ruin. Visitors who make the trek to the top of the hill are rewarded with a sweeping view over the town that spans the old town fortifications, the mighty Rhône and some of the more recent constructions including the compact 14,500 capacity Stade Tourbillon, home to Sion football club, which plays in the Swiss Super League and regularly features in European competitions.

Back in town, culture abounds, with museums of art, nature and archaeology, as well as the cantonal conservatoire where I stand for a short time to enjoy the music. Prominent but overshadowed by the structures on the hills is Cathédrale de Notre-Dame de Sion, which sits a few steps from Place de la Planta. The least visited of the three religious buildings, it nevertheless boasts elegant architecture and elaborate stained-glass windows, and is another impressive piece of work dating back to the fifteenth century.

Modern by comparison is the wine producer Bonvin, which is a mere 150 years old. It is, however, the oldest business of its kind in the Valais. Its origins lie in the early nineteenth century, when an ancestor of the founder returned from a trip to Bordeaux with vines in his luggage and ideas exercising his entrepreneurial mind. He used the environment around Sion as the framework for his wine business, eventually transforming the slopes adjacent to the town into substantial domaines. His grandson, Charles Bonvin, turned it into an enterprise that continues to thrive.

The current generation of the family has modernised it by combining with another of the town's winemaking institutions, Varone, to open Les Celliers de Sion. This is effectively a wine theme park, with numerous opportunities to learn about and taste some of the produce from around the region.

Among the activities is a walk through the vineyards along the Bisse de Clavau to discover the grape varieties that grow in this part of Switzerland. The bisses are regarded as symbolic of the perennial struggle that accompanies the cultivation of vines. They were created in a manner that allows water to be diverted onto the slopes. According to various versions of local legend, either the Romans or the Saracens were responsible for introducing the irrigation system to the area. By the start of the last century the network extended to 1,400 kilometres.

Meanwhile, inside the modernist building are various tasting choices, spanning self-service servings from an automatic dispenser to a sensory experience, which focuses on sight and sound to prove there is more to enjoying wine than an educated palate. There's also a huge shop, and eager purchasers stroll around, pens and order forms in hand, selecting bottles for their personal cellars or perhaps an upcoming life event.

And every Saturday Les Celliers de Sion is one of the nine stops on the itinerary for a wine bus, which drops thirsty visitors who want to try a few glasses. One of the stopping-off points is a wine bar in the middle of Sion, Verre à Pied, which is named after a stemmed wine glass. In the case of this bar, it might also refer to the fact that drinkers can stand at outdoor tables to enjoy a locally produced wine. In keeping with what I've seen elsewhere in Sion, 500 millilitre bottles feature prominently, and a typical glass size is 100 millilitres.

The bar is run by a group of sixteen producers and a wine broker, working under the title, Encaveurs de Sion. Among the members are several wineries whose products were on the wine list for the Marathon des Saveurs.

It's time for me to decide which wine I'll be taking home, so I study the options. I narrow my choice down to the most common grape varieties – Chasselas for white and Pinot Noir for red. I savour a glass of chilled Fendant before deciding that this will be the first bottle into my case. It is Fendant Sans Culotte – the name dating back to the time of the French Revolution, when the peasants who couldn't afford the same silk breeches worn by nobility were described as being 'without culottes'.

This wine took its title when Charles Bonvin decided to create what he saw as an innovative version of Fendant, making it in large concrete tanks rather than employing the established fermentation method. Given his revolutionary approach, he referred to the stories of the French Revolution and decided to use the name 'Sans Culotte'. In 1997, it won the prestigious Coupe Chasselas for the best Swiss wine made from that grape variety. It continues to be a popular choice on restaurant wine lists and in private cellars across the country.

The wine is pale yellow and has the slight fizz from residual gas that I noted when I tasted it previously. It is refreshing and fruity and excellent on its own as an aperitif, but I'm told is also great with fish and cheese, particularly raclette. As this bottle is made by Charles Bonvin, the name behind the Celliers de Sion, I like the connection that brings together various elements of my Swiss experience, so I buy this and pack it carefully into my case before setting off for home.

Switzerland has been fun. The people are kind and efficient, the landscape is stunning, helped admittedly by the fabulous weather, and the wine is excellent. After that inauspicious start with the yodeller on arriving in Sion, I have seen enough to dispel some of the Swiss stereotypes. I have also dipped my toe in Swiss history and the country's winemaking traditions.

I'm aware that stiffer tests lie ahead as I move on to competitive races. But it has been a pleasing start to my challenge, and I'm now looking forward to the next stage.

Glass half-full moment: Experiencing a spectacular route that was a good test of my fitness

Glass half-empty moment: Realising the event is less of a race than I had expected

Wine selected for Colin's Case: Bonvin Fendant Sans Culotte 2020

Two

SLOVENIA

TUNE OF THE DAY:
'The Tide is High' — Blondie

I'm so taken by Izola as I arrive on the bus from Ljubljana that I miss my stop. I realise my error as we leave the town behind and the number of pedestrians thins out. The driver manages to conceal her mirth at my schoolboy error then pulls in at the next available point and cheerily opens the luggage storage, allowing me to recover my bag.

She has deposited me at the top of the Strunjan cliff, a name I recognise from my pre-travel research. It will play an important part in my trip, particularly the race in which I'm taking part this weekend. Below me sits a quaint seaside town that juts into the Mediterranean like the island it once was — and from which it takes its name. Initially, a bridge linked Izola to the mainland. That changed in the nineteenth century when a wall surrounding the town was dismantled, with the resulting rubble used to fill the gap and join the two parts.

Clearly, my mental image of a rundown fishing town stripped of its former industrial glories was completely inaccurate and massively unkind. It is a clean, lively little place with striking architecture and, even in November, is obviously a destination for relaxation-seeking tourists, ranging from young families to pensioners, who stroll casually as they would in high season, albeit dressed in slightly more substantial clothes.

The colourful buildings topped with red tiled roofs are dominated by two church spires, and boats bob gently in the harbour. On appearance alone, it could be in Italy, the country a short distance along the coast to which it once belonged. The houses that sit proudly above the town as I head slowly back downhill to where I should have left the bus are also distinctly Italianate. However, for more than two decades this has been Slovenia, a young, vibrant nation that continues to grow in confidence and evolve economically.

Izola itself has an intriguing history. There is evidence of human life here dating back 250,000 years. It has gone from being an independent state with its own laws to form part of Slovenia, a land of stunning scenery, where past turmoil sits cheek-by-jowl with the vibrancy of what this country has become. Modern Slovenia escaped the control of Yugoslavia in 1990 when around eighty-eight per cent of its citizens voted for independence and, like a child freed from the steely grip of an overbearing parent, it has matured into something which is well-rounded, free-thinking and maturing at a measured pace.

My only previous visit to this part of the world was a couple of years before that vote when I spent a holiday along the coast. At that time, there were tensions on several levels and it was no surprise that the birth of Slovenia, the first of six republics to leave Yugoslavia, was accompanied by some pain, albeit mercifully brief. A ten-day war followed the move to become an independent country, but a peace deal ended the conflict. Slovenia joined the United Nations in May 1992 and became a member of the European Union in 2004.

Its coastline measures little more than the distance of a marathon and Izola is one of the towns that benefit from a seaside location. One of the first things to strike me is the ease with which everyone – from the woman in the bus station café to all public-facing staff in transport and hospitality – slips confidently into fluent English. It exposes my own limitations. I have learned a few words but acknowledge that my vocabulary is woefully inadequate to converse in Slovenian. As someone who has always been fascinated by language and languages, I am embarrassed to sheepishly start every conversation with the question, 'Do you speak English?', knowing, of course, that the answer will be in the affirmative. I soon discover that Izola's inhabitants won't hold it against me and are invariably keen to showcase their linguistic skills.

On my first visit to the main part of town, I note that the bell towers I saw from my initial vantage point belong to the Church of St Maurus – patron saint of Izola – and to the Church of St Mary of Alieto. Meanwhile, the narrow, cobbled streets and pastel house fronts fill tightly packed spaces that are reminiscent of some swankier fishing villages in other locations along the Mediterranean coast.

The Italian influence is also prominent when it comes to dining, with pizza and pasta restaurants predominantly the alternatives to places that serve fish caught nearby. Although locals are less reliant on the waters that surround them than they once were – a story that is told in the town's House of the Sea Museum – little boats still leave the harbour to seek a catch that will appear on menus the following day, and men can be seen fixing their nets in anticipation of the next excursion.

A gentle attitude to life prevails among residents who are friendly and welcoming. The Slovenian government is committed to making the country a green destination by developing a programme of responsible tourism. Places wishing to be included in the scheme must sign up to specific standards. The result is a focus on outdoor activities, sustainable food production and a constitution containing the right to clean drinking water. The number of trucks travelling in convoy-like groups during my bus journey from Ljubljana suggested that there is capacity for further improvement, but it is an admirable ambition and one which implies that this is a forward-looking nation.

The tourism marketers have been handed a gift as advertising campaigns highlight the letters l-o-v-e in the name Slovenia to promote the country. My own purpose this weekend is to avoid being the man who put the s-l-o into Slovenia.

I'm here for an event that combines tradition and modernity, the Martinov vinski tek. This is a wine run that takes its name from St Martin, who is celebrated on 11 November each year. I have signed up for one of the many festivities that take place across the country as Slovenians pay their respects to the fruits of autumn, particularly what is grown in vineyards.

Born in Hungary in the fourth century, St Martin was a soldier who converted to Christian orthodoxy and eventually became Bishop of Tours in France. Before taking on that appointment, he was forced into exile and, while travelling, sought shelter on the island of Gallinaria – the place now known as Izola. He then journeyed back to Tours where he was credited with being involved in introducing pruning to the winemaking process. That happened after he left his donkey tied to a row of vines. When he returned several hours later, the donkey had munched through the plants. The following year, those same plants flourished more than others nearby. The lesson was learned.

He was an influential character across various European countries, including the UK, where he gave his name to St Martin in the Fields Church in London's Trafalgar Square. He is now acclaimed in many parts of the world for achievements that reputedly include helping to develop winemaking in the region around Tours.

He is also represented in Madrid's Museo del Prado, which is home to a canvas, *The Wine of Saint Martin's Day*. It is the work of Pieter Bruegel the Elder and depicts a group of peasants celebrating the occasion. The painting is believed to be set in Belgium, but tells a story that is consistent with the Slovenian version of the saint, showing a group of people attempting to secure a share of the new wine.

Legend in Slovenia suggests that St Martin turns the must – a sludgy soup of grapes, skins, seeds and stems – into wine. This tradition is treated with reverence and the service of baptism is part of the celebrations that end with a feast traditionally featuring a goose stuffed with apples or chestnuts and red cabbage.

Costumed participants re-enact his contribution in towns and villages across the country in the lead-up to St Martin's Day, before sitting down to their meal. The blessing can be given only by a man dressed as a bishop, a priest or as St Martin himself. These celebratory events range from violin and accordion music to more energetic activities such as organised hikes across agricultural land as a way of cultivating an appetite for the feast that lies ahead.

The biggest celebration occurs in Maribor, the country's second city and home to a vine that is recorded in the *Guinness Book of Records* as the world's oldest. More than 400 years after it was planted, it still produces grapes that are made into wine. The vine even has a museum dedicated to its story.

The Slovenian passion for wine is not exclusive to Maribor. In addition to being an integral part of the lifestyle, winemaking clearly plays a big part in the country's economic success. That is reflected in the number of growers who permeate all walks of life. I have read that it is also represented in television programmes, with the most popular soap operas telling tales of wine dynasties and their tribulations. I'm sure that some of those workers will be competing in the series of races taking place this weekend.

The run that I have entered will start and finish in Izola. The Strunjan cliff, which I inadvertently encountered on arriving, and is home to a national park, is among the landmarks we will pass. The race was billed as ten kilometres when I submitted my online entry, but the pre-event documentation showed that this had grown to eleven, while the race profile suggests that it is a little longer than that. Despite the relatively short distance, there is nothing easy about it. Starting and finishing next to the harbour, it is a multi-surface circuit with all kinds of challenges including 170 metres of ascent. Having looked at previous results, I know it attracts a high standard of athlete, so the pace at the front of the field is likely to be quick. It's important that I don't get sucked into running too fast in the early stages as I will inevitably pay the price later for any such exuberance.

This is one run in a wider programme of the weekend's events in Izola that come under the umbrella of the Obala Trails series. In addition to the Martinov vinski tek, there is a choice of races over eighteen, thirty-three, sixty-three and eighty-seven kilometres. For those choosing the longer two, the action starts in the middle of the night. Competitors, who must carry bits and pieces of survival kit, are transported by bus to the starting point and will be seen back at the finish late in the evening.

The sight of the track-suited Slovenian national team holding a meeting in an outdoor café shortly after my arrival is a gentle reminder that, although this is a bit of fun for me, it's a much more serious undertaking for those at the peak of their athletic careers. Results will matter for some.

The races bring a late-season bonus for Izola's tourism industry, with hotels fully booked, a small village of camper vans springing up in a car park near the waterfront as the weekend approaches, and even signs of activity in the campsite above the town. With 700 runners, their families and supporters, as well as the race organisation team, they also deliver a boost to the coffers of bars and restaurants, which are thrumming at all hours.

Taking the more challenging runs as a reference point, it seems that I have plumped for the soft option. However, I'm in no doubt that a stern physical test lies ahead. It may be shorter than the event in Switzerland a few weeks ago, but I suspect this is going to be tougher.

Arriving at the start with plenty of time to spare, I decide to keep my legs moving with a gentle jog around the back streets. There I encounter a couple of serious-looking runners making their own final preparations. One of them – the part of his race number that is visible shows he is called Matej or something similar – looks like the kind of character that will feature at the head of the field. He is a muscular, barrel-chested powerhouse with a haircut that is distinctly Eastern European, shaved all over but with a long thatch on top, rather like a floppy Mohican style. I imagine that he may be one of the men who graft among the vines during the week. He certainly looks like a no-nonsense competitor.

While Matej completes his final warm-up, I head towards the start, where the group has started to gather. I may have lost what pace I once possessed as the years have taken their toll, but I have retained what passes as an athletic build and I am aware of some people eyeing up the stranger in town and possibly trying to assess whether I might pose a threat to those with podium aspirations. My linguistic inadequacies prevent me from putting them at ease. I haven't a clue what the Slovenian is for 'no need to worry about me, mate'.

In perfect conditions – autumn sunshine and a moderate breeze – a countdown sets the 200 or so runners entered for my race on their way. For most, the early pace is gentle, as the group proceeds along a narrow path leading to a metal bridge where the bunch clatters over in single file. I've walked along this part of the harbour side several times, so I know this opening segment will be flat before the course jolts brutally upwards.

With no stewards to act as guides, the runners need to be alert for the red-and-white tape attached to fences, hedges and lampposts, signalling the path we should be following. We have barely started to string out and I am just settling in to a regular pace when we pass through a park and the first group veers off the prescribed route. A girl beside me shouts the errant leaders back on track. She is urgently jabbing the screen of her phone, having downloaded the detailed circuit. Like schoolchildren admonished by their teacher, the culprits acknowledge their error and soon all is back in order.

We join the promenade where I strolled yesterday. It sits close to the water's edge and has no wall to separate land from sea. In contrast to when I passed this way previously, the waves are lapping gently over the concrete. Timing my stride is essential in order to keep my feet dry. Some in the group plough on regardless, happy to paddle in the water. Ahead, I see that the waves are becoming a little livelier, with foam rising above head height. When we reach that point, the footpath is submerged and the waves are washing over it, soaking many of the runners. There is no alternative to wet shoes, so I plough on and do my best to dodge the overhead deluge, which has become quite violent as the waves crash over the runners.

One man is channelling his inner King Canute and mounts a concrete bench, shouting at the water, which is deaf to his exhortations and continues to crash its waves over an increasingly bedraggled group of runners. I won't see him again, although I'm fairly sure he hasn't been washed away. For me, running through deep water is disconcerting rather than dangerous but it means that my shoes and socks are now soaked and a little uncomfortable as we escape up some steps.

Having seen the profile before I left home, and ambled around here, I know that the first climb looms. It's a draining hill that cuts through olive groves, each bend concealing the next seemingly interminable upward haul. Overall, it covers almost two kilometres, gaining more than 100 metres in altitude. Eventually the gradient relents and we reach the car park of a hotel, which is in the Strunjan Nature Reserve, sitting atop that infamous flysch cliff, which I now feel I know well.

However, the climb is not quite done and I can picture race organisers chuckling to themselves as they throw in another short, sharp test. We then move away from the tarmac to a gravel path, which edges gently higher before finally, with thighs and lungs burning, I reach the top. The girl with the phone shouts to a few runners ahead that they have strayed again, and another adjustment brings them back on track.

Farm paths lead to a short but gentle downhill section between olive trees before we return to a road that descends sharply. Somewhat worryingly, I see a bunch of around ten runners coming in the opposite direction. At the head of the group is Matej, and causing me further angst about what lies ahead is the fact that they are reduced to a walking pace. I will subsequently discover that he is one of the athletes competing over eighteen kilometres and we won't be climbing that particular hill, but for some time I have a nagging fear that we will come back to it later.

A roundabout at the foot of the hill is stewarded by police officers, who ensure everyone crosses unharmed to the safety of a hedge-lined lane used by cyclists and dog walkers. Its flatness offers some respite and gives everyone an opportunity to establish a steady stride. A glance at my watch shows that I am operating at what I consider to be a respectable pace as we approach the midpoint drinks station set up among vines that grow beside the path. Few competitors take advantage of what is on offer, but the encouragement of the people dispensing the water is timely as it becomes softer underfoot and similar to many of the cross-country courses I encountered in my youth.

Already depleted energy levels are further reduced as the glutinous surface calls for more nifty footwork, and even a return to a more solid surface offers little respite. Eventually, a gentle climb through vines adjacent to the path leads us back onto tarmac. A van parked at the junction bears the markings of Santomas, a winemaker that is among the main sponsors. A cheery young man standing at the roadside and wielding an uncorked bottle of red offers a sample. Stopping would not be a good idea right now. It's an easy decision to decline. It seems I'm not alone in thinking this way as the others around me have a similar reaction.

We climb a little further and leave the road once more, but we're still on solid ground and a 200-metre-long tunnel comes into view. This is part of the Parenzana cycle path. It has been created from a disused railway that originally linked Trieste in Italy with Poreč in Croatia, but closed in 1935. It reopened in 2006 as a 123-kilometre track.

We emerge from the tunnel then turn into a built-up part of Izola, which I don't recognise, then hit a descent that offers some relief. I glance at my watch and realise that I am moving well and I manage to reel in a couple of those ahead of me. I then notice that I am passing my hotel, so the feeling of disorientation disappears and I have a reasonable idea of what lies between here and the finishing line.

The runners around me turn right towards the town centre and I follow. Once more the phone-wielding expert points out that we are not adhering to the official course, and that the red-and-white tape lies directly in front. I'm fortunate that she is running at the same pace as I am, otherwise I would almost certainly have added significantly to the total distance. The group re-forms and we head back towards the waterside. This time there is no need to run through the sea, although I note that the waves are still splashing over the surface of the promenade as we head in the opposite direction and back towards the harbour.

In the distance, I see the bars and cafés, crammed with people enjoying the warm weather and sipping cool thirst-quenchers that are tantalisingly alluring right now. Tiredness strikes and I am comforted by the rattle of the metal bridge as we retrace our earlier steps. Then comes the welcome sight of the inflatable finishing line and the accompanying tunes being blasted out by the DJ.

His selection may not be music to my ears, but there is a sense of relief as I stumble over the line. Again I resist the temptations of the Santomas wine man, who has a tasting stall set up. Instead, some water and an energy drink start the recovery from the hardest run I have experienced for a while. It has been tough going at times, but I feel exhilarated. My objective was to enjoy the experience and perform reasonably well. Overall, I'm happy that I have achieved both of those aims. I don't want to be results-driven, but inherent competitiveness is a difficult flame to extinguish and I can't help but take a peek when the names flash up on a massive screen provided by Philips, the main sponsor, and I see that I achieved a top-forty finishing spot that makes me particularly satisfied with my efforts.

Despite my fatigue, I am conscious that my race was the short version. Finishers in the longer event are intermingled with the stragglers from the Martinov vinski tek. Some have clearly taken it seriously, others less so, and I smile at those who celebrate their achievement with a cigarette – indeed one pairs his smoke with a bottle of beer. Well, he earned it.

And so to the next phase of my visit, the research and decision about the next bottle to merit inclusion in my case. Slovenia has three wine-growing regions, each blessed with different soils and climates that mean there are fifty-two grape varieties, all of which thrive in their immediate environment. Izola is in Primorska, which is divided into four districts. The town sits in Slovenian Istria, which is further split into two sub-districts – coastal and inland. The first of these, where I currently am, includes the Milje Hills, Tinjan, the Rižana Valley, and other areas which benefit from Mediterranean attributes, including very little frost and high levels of rainfall.

Although around seventy per cent of the sixty million or so vines in Slovenia produce white wine, Primorska is best known for reds. The soil is of the *terra rossa* variety, meaning it is rich brown in colour thanks to the tradition of deep ploughing. The varieties are also dictated to some extent by the climate. Rainfall is apparently considerably higher than the average I experience in Edinburgh and this, combined with hot summers, produces the high-quality grapes that are driving the growth in demand for Slovenian wines, both abroad and at home, where it's common to see bars filled with drinkers ordering a glass of white rather than a beer.

While there are many wineries around here, some stand out for their longevity and innovation. One such business is Zaro, an institution in Izola, with hilltop vines and olive groves, as well as a great wine bar that takes its name, Manzioli, from the square where it is located in the ground floor of a former palace. The bar is described as an extension of the company's wine cellar, meaning I can sample its top produce without needing to climb the surrounding hills.

There's also a Zaro boat berthed in the harbour, confirming the family's other tradition as fishermen. The boat is now used for trips along the coastal waters that present guests with a view of the vines from a different angle and tips on how to pair wine with fish.

In addition to applying their skills at sea, the Zaros have been producing wine and olive oil since the family settled here in 1348. Responsibility for preserving the heritage currently rests with Matej Zaro, who takes his duties seriously. He is helped in that regard by the gods, who have endowed him with fertile slopes that enjoy the perfect climatic conditions to grow grapes and olives. Among the attributes are the flysch soils that are the perfect foil to the winemaker's talents when it comes to creating organic wines. Matej has enhanced those attributes with modern techniques that draw on global developments in the industry.

While following the local trend for great reds, Zaro is also a renowned producer of whites and rosés, as well as being a big proponent of orange wines. The predominant grape variety in the area is Refošk, but the Manzioli bar also serves top-notch wines made from Malvazija, Negratenera, Merlot and Cabernet Sauvignon. They are produced using what is referred to as minimal intervention. That means allowing them to develop naturally and with limited involvement from the winemaker. Fermentation is also left to occur in the cellar without too much human interference.

Zaro now boasts several vineyards, each producing grape varieties that thrive in the specific regional conditions. The company's vineyards and olive groves above Izola offer views along Slovenia's Istrian coast towards Trieste, with the brooding backdrop of the Alps and, on a clear day, the Dolomites offering a spectacular framework within which Matej and his team strive for constant improvement.

After returning briefly to the hotel for a shower and a change of clothing, I head back to the harbour side. I decide that the perfect place to sample the fruits of the Zaro labours is the wine bar. Before doing so, I have another opportunity to speak to the man from Santomas, who is still at his stall near the finishing line. He tells me that this too is a long-established business, now in the capable hands of its sixth generation of winemakers. It's based in Šmarje, a little way outside Izola, and relies heavily on tradition. The current incumbent is the first female at the helm, and as he pours the wine, the man from Santomas enthusiastically endorses her approach, promising an exciting future for the company.

I ask to taste his Malvazija, which proves to be light and refreshing and made following a similar method to the one used to produce orange wine. He offers a mild rebuke over my pronunciation, pointing out that my emphasis on the second syllable is used in Croatia, while Slovenians emphasise the third. I make a mental note – Mal-va-zeeah it is.

With the wine tasting attracting an increasingly enthusiastic crowd as runners from the various races regain their composure after their earlier exertions and seek out a glass of something that is the reward they have grafted for, I decide to carry on my Slovenian wine education elsewhere and head for Manzioli Square.

Matej Zaro is such a fan of orange wine that he helps to organise a festival each spring in Izola. If marmite is regarded as the benchmark for divided opinion, then orange wine is surely a sibling of the beef-flavoured beverage. For many, it is a noteworthy addition to a wine market where product innovation is limited. To others, it is barely worth the considerable effort that its production demands.

Maceration is the distinguishing feature of making orange wine. This effectively uses red wine processes in the production of whites, which are typically made by squeezing the juice from grapes and then fermenting the liquid alongside any additives. Some of those who grow Malvazija, particularly in European countries such as Slovenia, Croatia and Italy, believe the wine takes on supplementary qualities when the grape skins form part of the process, adding flavour and colour. The technique, which is also being adopted in New Zealand and the US, is a standard step in making red wine, but has only recently come back into fashion for whites, having been used on occasions in the past before falling from favour.

The maceration – also called skin contact – extracts colour and flavour from the skins and results in a deep yellow wine that often becomes orange and has flavours of herbs as well as some tannin. The juice and skins may be left together for up to six months, although shorter periods are common, sometimes as brief as a day or two.

I accept a recommendation from a member of the bar staff and start with a glass of the 2018 orange wine. It comes with a glowing endorsement that this is a house speciality. Sadly, it leaves me underwhelmed. Instead, I move on to Malvazija Pivol 2020, a maceration-light white wine, where the skins are left in the juice for only a short time. This is an entirely different proposition – fruity, refreshing and utterly delicious. It is golden, medium-bodied and dry and is served perfectly chilled in the relaxed atmosphere of the bar, which boasts a pared back indoor space. Customers can also sit on concrete benches at upturned barrels used as tables outside in the historic square.

Pivol is one of Zaro's four vineyards around Izola. The others are in Folo, Roncaldo and Morer, giving the family coastal and inland coverage and broadening out the range of wine styles.

I believe the selection for my case is made, but just to reassure myself, I decide to try a red. I ask for a recommendation, and I receive a glass of Folo Rosso from a member of staff who also gives a full history and detailed explanation of its attributes. This, too, is a delicious wine that brings together twenty per cent Cabernet Sauvignon and eighty per cent Merlot grapes. It is smooth and makes a strong argument for a place in my dozen picks. But ultimately, it is pipped at the post by the white.

Other contenders included Refošk. This is a red I tasted with food and which I found to be an excellent match for beef. It was light, fresh and fruity but, for me, less enjoyable than the Folo Rosso.

With my decision finalised, and the bottle purchased, I enjoy a stroll around town. I pass a specialist wine shop I visited earlier in my stay. The owner explained to me that she works with smaller makers that produce limited amounts of boutique wines. Meanwhile, supermarkets tend to sell the produce of a large wine co-operative that is based ten minutes away. This is an insight into where the Slovenian wine industry sits in its domestic market – a large number of players producing high-quality wines from small plots, and a few large companies dominating the retail and export markets, notably to South Korea, Japan and the US.

Later in the day, the action moves to a nearby park, which takes its name from the former Izola resident Pietro Coppo, a geographer and cartographer who produced an atlas of the world in the sixteenth century. This is where the presentation for the race takes place. I am strolling towards the venue when I notice Matej arrive. I assume he is heading there to pick up an award, and I congratulate myself on my ability to identify a top performer.

My shortcomings in Slovenian prevent me from following the proceedings in detail, but several runners make multiple visits to the podium. Among the winners is a lady with whom I had a race-long tussle before finally overtaking her in the closing stages. She wins what I believe is the veteran women's race. A younger guy who crossed the line one place ahead of me is also rewarded for his efforts, although I don't know what category he has won.

The variable shapes and sizes of those who can succeed as trail runners is confirmed when a sturdy man in chinos and a woollen sweater, looking like an old-school bank manager who has just stepped off the golf course, emerges from the crowd to accept the prize for taking top spot in the veterans' category over eighteen kilometres. The ceremonies drag on much longer than the advertised half-hour. Alas my predictive skills have proved faltering, as Matej disappears into the late afternoon gloom empty-handed.

The festival of running concludes in the evening with what is dubbed a Mega concert featuring a local group called Mambo Kings. The Mega label was also applied to the eve-of-race pasta party, which was perfectly adequate but fell some way short of justifying that adjective. I adjust my musical expectations accordingly. The four lads in the band are hitting their stride as I reach the open-air cinema where the gig is taking place. It sounds like more of the cover versions that are the soundtrack in virtually every restaurant I have visited, as well as being the tunes blasted out on radio programmes that offer background entertainment during bus journeys. I decide there's only so much Europop I can take. I bow out early, content to bring an end to a memorable day in which the highlight was a fabulously varied and arduous run that introduced me to part of the landscape where grapes are grown for some of the wines I wanted to explore.

The return bus journey to Ljubljana is by a circuitous route that shows me some of the country's spectacular scenery, the villages and towns where the St Martin celebrations will take place over the coming week or so, and some parts of the country that have not yet been exposed to the progress seen elsewhere in Slovenia. The cost of my fare is a couple of euros. My fellow passengers span the age spectrum and include what I assume to be a young student who has just enjoyed a weekend with the family and is loading a wooden box stuffed with fruit and vegetables into the luggage space.

In the final hours before I leave, I scratch the surface of Ljubljana, a capital city that is cosmopolitan, steeped in history and a popular destination for international tourists.

Overall, it has been an intriguing trip. I've even picked up a few local words. So, 'hvala' Slovenia. Thanks for a demanding wine run in a wonderful landscape, and for your friendly welcome. And thank you for the introduction to your wine.

Glass half-full moment: A challenging race and great introduction to Slovenian wine

Glass half-empty moment: Hanging around at bus stations owing to off-season timetables

Wine selected for Colin's Case: Zaro Malvazija Pivol 2020

Three

ITALY

TUNE OF THE DAY:
'Slip Slidin' Away' – Paul Simon

I have reasons to celebrate. The landmark birthday that provided the spark for this project is just a couple of weeks away, with my wife's birthday and Christmas falling a few days either side of that. Celebrations and bubbly are unquestionable partners, so concluding my year with a trip to Prosecco country seems apt.

Prosecco is what Italy brings to the party when fizz is called for. It has been the cork-popping choice for many Brits over the past two decades. In fact, in the mid-2010s, drinkers in the UK were quaffing around a quarter of all the Prosecco produced by Italy's winemakers. Demand was so high that quality began to suffer in the rush to satisfy thirsty customers and profit from the trend. There was also a frenzy of grape planting and the amount of land in the Veneto region that was used to grow vines increased by around eighty per cent over a five-year period.

Many litres of hastily produced bubbles threatened to flood the market – especially in the UK – and damage

51

the reputation of a product that had been admired for its excellence, its status as a challenger to champagne in the sparkling wine stakes, and for the fact that it was generally a little less expensive than its French counterpart. However, driving prices even lower and the dwindling standards being employed by some of the money-chasing winemakers combined to harm Prosecco's standing.

Concerned at the longer-term impact on exports, as well as the damage caused to the environment – not to mention the health of plants and people – by the increased use of pesticides to stimulate production levels, some of the more reputable makers worked with the authorities to tighten the rules and raise standards.

Among the responses was a focus on the classifications that define the product. The result was a move in 2009 towards greater clarity by placing better-quality Prosecco into one of two groups – DOC (Denominazione di Origine Controllata), which is less strict, or DOCG (Denominazione di Origine Controllata e Garantita), which covers wine made in a limited area across the regions of Veneto and Friuli Venezia Giulia. These categorisations help buyers, although, as is the case with similar systems in other countries, they are largely the outcome of box-ticking exercises, and the standard of the finished product depends on the individual producers.

The main grape variety is Glera, which was known as the Prosecco grape until it adopted a new identity as part of the 2009 makeover. In some cases, Glera is combined with other grapes, which are allowed to account for up to fifteen per cent of the total.

Winemaking in the town of Prosecco, near Trieste, dates back to the mid-thirteenth century, although records suggest it has been going on for more than 2,000 years, with Livia, wife of the Emperor Octavian Augustus, said to have reached an advanced age with the help of the health-boosting features of wine from that area. These days, total annual production within the two Prosecco categories is around 500 million bottles.

I'm wondering whether I will be able to distinguish between run-of-the-mill Prosecco and the superior offerings. I hope to learn more about the places and the processes, as well as sampling some of the fabled produce during my final trip of the year. My palate has led me to Vidor for a run through some of the vineyards that produce DOCG-rated Prosecco.

I have never visited this part of Italy and my only knowledge of Treviso is thanks to Benetton Rugby, which competes in the same league as Edinburgh and Glasgow Warriors. There's no action at the green-and-white bedecked Stadio Comunale di Monigo this weekend. That's because the biancoverdi are in Scotland for a game against Edinburgh. Glasgow had a game here a week ago – unfortunate timing, as a reversal of the fixtures would have meant being able to combine the run with some rugby watching. The important relationship between sport and wine is underlined by the fact that Benetton's sponsors include Prosecco DOC, the umbrella organisation that supports many of the local sparkling wine producers.

My base is around thirty kilometres from Treviso, the provincial capital, and is within walking distance of Valdobbiadene, which is the administrative base for Prosecco makers. While I wouldn't claim to be a proficient Italian speaker, I can understand some of what is written or said. The limited confidence I have in my ability to converse in the language takes a bit of a dent when I ask at the bus station for details of the 110 service to Valdobbiadene and stumble over the pronunciation – if only I had managed to reserve a room in Vidor.

During the journey, the bus heads towards the snow-capped peaks, which watch over an area that was named a United Nations World Heritage Site in 2019. Passengers hop aboard for short journeys as we pass through towns where honey-coloured stone buildings are the construction style of choice. I am sitting behind the driver and I'm conscious of stares I'm receiving from an elderly woman, who has just got on and is directly across the aisle from me. It strikes me that I have perhaps taken the seat she normally occupies. She gets off at the next village, so I'm spared any further attention.

The one-hour trip offers me a glimpse of daily life in a part of the world I have only ever witnessed while following the Giro d'Italia cycle race on television each year. As with many European countries, use of public transport is encouraged, and my fare is covered by the two-day pass that is included with the transfer from the airport into central Treviso.

While tourists are lured here for walking, skiing, mountain biking and, obviously, wine tasting, there are few hotels. Much of the accommodation is based on Italy's *agriturismo* model, which offers rooms attached to farms or, around here, wineries and is a government-supported project to repurpose unused or unprofitable agricultural land and buildings for holiday lettings.

With the limited available space in Vidor already snapped up when I started looking for a room, I am booked into the Locanda Sandi, a delightful old house owned by a winemaking family and run by fabulously friendly staff. It's around five kilometres from the race venue. So, that's my warm-up sorted.

The run will pass four wineries as the route rises and dips over the rugged mountainous terrain which features a collection of hogback hills and farmland that will be demanding, even in favourable conditions. The landscape is, nonetheless, stunning.

The economy of Vidor, which sits on the Piave river, relies heavily on the wine industry, as well as several thriving businesses that make furniture for homes and offices. The town's population of less than 4,000 is predominantly elderly. Viewed in decade-defined groups, the largest number of residents are aged over seventy, and records show that in 2016, there were three centenarians in the town. Perhaps that's another sign of the health-giving qualities of Prosecco claimed by the emperor's wife a couple of millennia ago.

The town was a pivotal site during the First World War, and its role is reflected in a tourist trail and a spectacular war memorial church that sits high above the town and houses the remains of Vidor's fallen soldiers in its crypt. I will have a close-up view, as it features on the run.

When I visit on Saturday, the streets are quiet, with the only signs of activity being a trickle of shoppers emerging with trollies from the supermarket, which sits in a more modern part of town, and a group of workmen applying the final touches to the finishing gantry for the race. Despite this being December, handfuls of townsfolk occupy outside tables to enjoy a late-morning coffee or a pre-lunch aperitif in one of the cafés just off the main road, which is busy with passing traffic.

Meanwhile, a peloton of club cyclists heads for the hills, and moving in the opposite direction are walkers and hikers armed with sticks as a sign of the seriousness with which they approach their activity. The grape harvest is complete for the year, but there is still work to be done, and small groups of workers are clipping dead branches from the vines and tidying up the vineyards. Some are rolling out lengths of wire. A method, known as *bellussera*, which is popular around here, involves using wires attached to wooden poles to train the vines in a manner that allows grapes to be picked by hand, and I assume that this out-of-season activity in the fields is something to do with that.

The main race of the weekend is the Prosecco Run, a half-marathon, which normally boasts a field bristling with talent and this time includes athletes who have competed at the Olympics, as well as some high-performing African-born athletes who have made Italy their home and will race in the colours of local teams. However, the arduous course rules out personal best times for the 1,200 or so who will glance excitedly, or with trepidation, towards the peaks that tomorrow will taunt the runners as they head for La Tordera winery, where the town's mayor will give the starting signal. My original plan was to test myself over the half-marathon, although I'm not sure I'm ready for a run of this intensity. Instead, I have opted for the ten kilometre run, which bears the title, La Prosecchina, and is less demanding.

La Tordera is a place that looks worthy of some investigation. For more than a century, the Vettoretti family has been at the helm of this business, which strives to work in a manner that is consistent with modern vinification methods but retains strong links to the environment and tradition. The winery takes its name from a hill in the Cartizze area that featured a rock commonly called Tordera. The rock no longer exists, but La Tordera has gone from strength to strength and is now run by three siblings, who are the founder's great-grandchildren. The way this winery has evolved looks like an interesting story and I decide that it's a good place to seek a contender for the latest spot in my case of wine.

I have come to Vidor to check out the town and register for the race. The desks will be staffed from 2pm, so it seems good use of my time to book a half-hour tasting at La Tordera just before that. It's perhaps not textbook preparation for a running event, but I don't expect my vineyard experience to involve drinking large amounts.

I'm met by Athos, an Italian of German descent, who has a Greek name and speaks excellent English. He suggests that I taste four wines based on their sugar levels. This strikes me as an unusual approach to tasting, but it's a part of the process that's often overlooked, so I'm fascinated to learn more. The amount of sugar a bottle of Prosecco contains can vary considerably. At La Tordera it covers a range from zero to thirty-two grammes per litre. Athos places this in context by pointing out that some dessert wines can contain 100 grammes. At his suggestion, I will start at the lower end and work upwards.

He explains that the company makes wine that falls within the higher quality DOCG classification, meaning it comes from an area measuring around twenty-five kilometres between Valdobbiadene and Conegliano, and also produces some of the more widely available DOC. This uses grapes from vines that cover land that is around thirty times larger, is flatter, and extends from Venice to Trieste in four provinces of Friuli Venezia Giulia and five of Veneto. Wine falling into the first of these categories is distinguished by its brown seal around the top of the bottle, as opposed to the blue seal of those in the DOC group.

Athos tells me that sugar-free Prosecco is growing in popularity, especially among diners in restaurants as the ideal accompaniment to a meal, particularly seafood. It is fermented for longer to remove the sweetness, and this increases the alcohol level, although even at twelve per cent, it remains lower than many still wines. I try two others that contain eight grammes, then one with a higher level, making it an ideal aperitif.

I notice that some of the bottles, particularly at the higher-quality end, are closer to the shape I would associate with traditional wine than what I would expect from Prosecco bottles. Athos explains that this is an evolving trend, driven by complaints from restaurants, which felt the dumpier normal style took up too much space in their fridges.

He goes on to say that the recently completed harvest was good in terms of quality, although grape quantities were a little lower than the levels that have been typical of recent years. The key to a successful vintage is the absence of hail and avoiding too much rain at vital stages in the growth cycle. In addition, Athos points to the role of global warming in the life of a winemaker. Grapes are ripening quicker than they did historically and harvests have been brought forward, now taking place a full month earlier than they did five decades ago.

My own subsequent research reveals that newly harvested grapes are made into still wine after around twenty days of reacting to the yeast that is added. The wine undergoes a second fermentation to produce the bubbles, and the temperature of the wine is gradually reduced before the liquid is eventually bottled.

It has been an absorbing lesson from an expert and I feel I have been educated. Keeping my options open for when I may eventually choose to drink the wine, I select one that can be served before or alongside food. That narrows my choice to two bottles. I taste each of them and surprise myself by managing to distinguish between wines that are ostensibly the same, but which fall into each of the two categorisations. I like the smoothness and fully rounded taste of the higher-quality DOCG Brunei Brut, which will take its place in my case.

La Tordera owns several vineyards, but Brunei is made using grapes grown in Vidor, around 180 metres above sea level. It is pale in colour and has strong flavours of apple and pear. This wine is available in seven sizes, ranging from a half-bottle to a hefty twelve-litre monster – known as a Balthazar – which, I guess, would slake even the most persistent of thirsts. The available space in my suitcase dictates that I buy the standard size.

It occurs to me that Brunei is an unusual name for an Italian product. It transpires that many centuries ago, plum trees grew where the vineyard now sits and the name Brunei is an evolution of the Latin word *pruni*, meaning plums.

As Athos returns from the shop, I ask about the vintage not appearing on the front label. This is common, he says, although it is shown in some cases. He then turns the bottle to show a grid of data that includes the year 2020 in small print, as well as a strip that reveals the sugar level – this wine contains eight grammes, placing it in the Brut category. Also on the label is confirmation that the grapes are hand harvested at a family farm, which has an environmentally friendly approach including the use of solar energy and low CO_2. The label is printed on recycled paper, and the bottles are made from recycled glass.

Athos wishes me well with my run, which will start at the back of the winery, and I set off for the race headquarters where there is a warm welcome as I register and pick up my competitor's wristband, particularly on the news that I have travelled from Scotland to run.

I wake to the sound of rain beating relentlessly against my window. I peer cautiously outside and see that puddles have formed overnight and the cars squelching through the surface water have their windscreen wipers in full clearance mode. I check the forecast, which offers hope, with the prediction that the rain will relent around the race start time, although it will be back later, possibly as snow.

The two alarms I've set are not needed – fear of oversleeping invariably leads to not sleeping at all – and a light breakfast later,

I set off with plenty of time to spare. Thankfully, conditions are easing when I leave the hotel for my jog/walk to Vidor. I stop off along the way to buy today's edition of the local newspaper. This is something I've done for each of my runs so far, and means I'll have a reminder of what was happening during my visits, even when, in the not-too-distant future, newspapers have ceased to be published in physical form. I tuck my copy of *Il Gazzettino* into my tiny backpack in which I carry keys, some cash, my mini video camera, which I use as a mobile notebook, and, in this case, gloves and hat.

La Prosecchina is described as an amateur race. However, replacing a race number with a coloured wristband does not mean it is easy. Its status has clearly not deterred some useful-looking athletes, togged out in the kit of various athletics and triathlon clubs, as the runners prepare to get started a few minutes later than scheduled from the yard behind La Tordera.

The course follows a path through vines and passes many of Vidor's landmark buildings, rising high above the town then swooping downwards and finishing on one of the few flat stretches, back at the community centre, which is the organisational hub for the day.

It's an opportunity for runners from the surrounding towns and villages to catch up, and one group, featuring what looks like a husband and wife, are in jovial mood as they complete their preparations. A drone hovers overhead, eliciting reactions that range from head-down refusal to acknowledge its presence to frantic waving as if seeking rescue from a desert island.

Then, as the starting countdown sends the runners on their way, I'm somewhere in the middle of a field of more than 500 runners. A gentle first kilometre passes by easily, leading through streets lined by residents who are standing by their doors with an eye out for friends and family, and possibly wondering what possessed these people to spend their Sunday morning in this way.

The first climb is a rude awakening. It follows a track through some vines. The grassy middle segment is relatively easy to negotiate, but the lanes on either side are muddy as a result of the overnight rain. Understandably, the central path is the choice of all but a few and it soon becomes congested, meaning everyone is forced to travel at the pace of the slowest individual. It's unfortunate that she has chosen to take a rest, and there is a release of built-up frustration as the followers pass on both sides as soon as that becomes possible. Ahead, runners in brightly coloured jackets are filed out in the form of a vibrant snake illuminating the day as they edge higher up the hill in single file.

Then, as I slither towards the perimeter of a path and teeter on the brink of falling into the adjacent vines, I am hammered from behind by a runner whose braking skills have been neutralised by the mud. Thankfully, she is slightly built and bounces sideways rather than shunting me into the undergrowth. The cloying underfoot conditions bring to mind that recurring nightmare that features attempts to flee a dangerous pursuer, only to find that an escape is thwarted by the slippery ground that prevents any traction.

The path swings violently from sharp climb to slithering

descent, defying all hope of establishing a rhythm. The few flat bits we encounter are boggy and offer little respite or hope of lengthening the stride. As is usually the case in a run of this type, those of similar ability quickly form into small groups that will travel at the same pace throughout the event and create some form of bond. Some will drop off and others will arrive as they recover from overcautious starts, but the core will remain largely intact.

Our collection of runners includes the couple who enlivened the pre-race activities. They wear the kit of an athletics club in Vedelago, a few miles from here, and are clearly legendary in the community. He is called Marco. The cheers that acknowledge his efforts, and his lively response to the urgings from those who have climbed one of the many hills to offer encouragement, illustrate that he is a character of some renown in Vidor.

A gentle ascent is a precursor to the next steep climb, this time thankfully on a solid road. However, it is a short sharp incline to the Col Castello, which enjoys spell-binding views over the town. Once the site of a castle that was destroyed in the sixteenth century, it now houses a war memorial to the townsfolk who fell in a bloody First World War battle here between Italian troops and the Austro-Hungarian army.

There is a rare and brief flattening of the surface, before another bottleneck occurs around the halfway point as we descend towards the Ca' Dal Molin winery. On this occasion, the reason for the build-up of bodies is a roadside table that is luring athletes to halt and sample the produce. Some runners stop for a chat and a taste, but, although I take the small glass that is thrust into my hand and enjoy its contents, I prefer not to break what rhythm I have established so, like my Prosecco, I am soon gone.

I suspect that Marco and his wife have chosen to linger a little longer, as they disappear from the group. Indeed, it thins out to a single file. Ahead of me is a runner from Venice Athletics Club, according to his top. He is named Paulo and is running with a mate, Stefano, who is behind me. Banter is flying from one to the other. It's over my head, in more ways than one – I haven't a clue what they are saying. Stefano overtakes me then he leaves his pal and disappears into the distance. I, too, will overtake Paulo later in the race.

We have now completed more than three-quarters of the distance and, according to the massive yellow sign at the side of the path, the organisers have decided that this is an appropriate time to warn runners that the conditions are dangerous. I am already aware of the need to be totally focused. Rarely have I had to concentrate so intensely on where I'm placing my feet.

We emerge into another winery. This is the Daldin estate, a name I recognise from having passed it on my way to the start of the race. Another offer of Prosecco has been rebuffed by most, although one group has decided to halt for another refreshment. Paulo and I decline and veer left before being directed to the next section, which takes us through a cowshed on the Ponte Vecchio farm. Grazing cattle stick their heads quizzically between the railings for a better view of the bizarre sight as runners traverse their terrain and exit at the other end of the shed.

It's flat around here, but the challenges are not yet done. A narrow bridge knocked together using planks of wood has been placed over a fast-flowing body of water. I clatter over it, then hear the rat-a-tat of footsteps that tell me someone is approaching quickly. A runner in Venice Triathlon kit blazes past, not to be seen again. I wonder why he has been behind me all this way when clearly he has a lot left in the tank.

Our route merges with that of the half-marathon for the final couple of kilometres. Runners who will feature among the leading finishers in the longer event whizz past as they grapple with the closing stages of their run. By this point I'm aware that we are covering more than ten kilometres. I trudge up one last rise, halfway between walking and trying to dredge a final effort from my tiring limbs before enjoying the relief as I reach the summit.

I gather pace descending the Col Marcon, another important site in the town's military history, and pass the Benedictine Abbey of Santa Bona before a final circuit through a flat segment of vines. Runners separate into finishing funnels, depending on the race they have contested, with the leading finishers in the half-marathon deservedly receiving greater attention.

A final flourish sees me over the line and a glance at my watch shows that it was actually just over eleven kilometres rather than the advertised distance. The definition of an amateur race means that results can't be published, and the time I have recorded is slower than I might have expected. However, the gruelling conditions have played their part, and I'm satisfied with my outing.

I recover my breath and collect drinks to help kick-start my rehydration. Back in the administration centre, preparations are underway for the presentations and, this being Italy, squads of helpers are serving dishes of pasta. I'm not ready to eat right now, so I decide to call it a day. I'm heading towards the exit when a crowd in front of me parts and I see a man with a camera. I guess he is from local television seeking the views of those who have completed the runs. And, as I move closer, I discern the familiar figure of Marco, who is being interviewed. He is loving it and his wife struggles for a share of the airtime.

The early start means I can get back to the hotel, shower and change, and still visit the centre of Valdobbiadene before it gets dark. The absence of pavements beside many of the roads means that, to my mind at least, pedestrians are at risk of being flattened by speeding traffic. I stroll the short distance and find a town that has clearly enjoyed affluence in the past and presumably still does given its status as the administrative capital for many Prosecco makers.

The eighteenth-century bell tower of the Santa Maria Assunta Cathedral casts its shadow over the main square, Piazza Marconi, and there are cafés with a feeling of tradition and permanence. There are even hotels, which I assume are used by those visiting the town on wine business. However, there isn't a great deal of activity. This is Sunday afternoon. Perhaps it gets busier on Mondays. That's certainly the case in Treviso, as I arrive in mid-morning the following day having again travelled on the number 110 bus. My flight home awaits.

Italy has been good, the Prosecchina was a blast, and the people, particularly at my accommodation, have been wonderful. Had I not been pursuing my goal of running around Europe to create a case of wine, I probably would never have chosen to visit this region. I'm sold on its attractions and look forward to another visit in future. So, arrivederci Valdobbiadene – I'll brush up on my Italian before my next trip.

Glass half-full moment: Discovering an area brimming with tradition and great wine

Glass half-empty moment: A malfunction by my camera (operator) means no race video

Wine selected for Colin's Case: La Tordera, Brunei DOCG 2020

Four

ENGLAND

TUNE OF THE DAY:
'Country House' — Blur

I'm ready to pull the cork on the first run of the new year. I already have my case quarter full and now I'm set to complete the remaining spaces by visiting more of Europe's most picturesque, captivating and historic wine locations and exploring what they have to offer. I've chosen to start this latest phase in a country that draws both praise and controversy in the world of vinification. I'm in England.

Global warming is playing a big part in winemaking, and nowhere is this more obvious than where I'm standing. You don't need to be an environmental activist to know that core temperatures have risen over recent decades. That trend has prompted owners in some wine heartlands to plant vines that are more resistant to heat and harsher growing conditions as a way of future-proofing their business. Changing climatic conditions also mean that regions previously considered unsuitable are now ideal for producing great wines. They are pushing the geographical limitations further north, transforming places that were once too cold or too wet into ideal vineyard locations. However, there has been some resistance. Some of the old-school winemakers in traditional markets are reluctant to acknowledge the arrival of the interlopers, meaning English wine gets mixed reviews. That's what makes this place so interesting.

During the period from 1989–2013, temperatures in southern England were similar to those of the Champagne region in the thirty years up to 1990. The two areas also have similar soil, so it's easy to see why environmental change is significant for English winemakers. Evidence shows a blossoming industry around the British Isles, with more than 700 vineyards – the smallest having only six vines, while Denbies, my current location, is at the other end of the scale with around 270 acres.

That said, attributing the growth in popularity of English wine exclusively to global warming is inaccurate. There is skill involved. To suggest that rising temperatures automatically result in a better product is just as unfair as suggesting that a talented photographer takes great snaps because he has a good camera, or a proficient chef cooks up a storm in the kitchen because he's using top-of-the-range pans. Clearly, the grapes are thriving, but the task of capitalising on that rests squarely with the winemaker. During this visit, I'm hoping to find out a little more about the essential skills and the role Denbies plays in helping English wine to prosper.

Denbies sits just outside Dorking, a market town less than an hour south of London by train, yet a world away from the hustle and bustle of city life. With one or two exceptions, the town appears to have largely avoided the invasion of national chains of shops and restaurants. Antique stores jostle for the attention of shoppers, with boutiques and art galleries adding to the quaintness of the place, while estate agents, hairdressers and tattoo artists also do a brisk trade.

The town is the birthplace of the actor Laurence Olivier, it was where the composer Ralph Vaughan Williams grew up, and it featured in the works of Jane Austen and Charles Dickens. A nearby church was used in the 1990s film, *Four Weddings and a Funeral*, and the town has been the scene of various television programmes including the sci-fi series, *Blakes Seven*, which I recall being an unmissable weekly event in my student house.

The land here in the Surrey hills boasts chalky soil and south-facing slopes. That makes it perfect for creating great wine. The buildings that occupy the Denbies site went through various phases before the land became the estate that it is today.

The records show that this plot and the buildings that sit on it take their name from John Denby, who built the original property in the mid-sixteenth century. In his book *The House on the Hill: The Story of Ranmore and Denbies*, S.E.D. Fortescue explains that the estate was also sometimes referred to as Denby's and Denbighs. According to Mona, the guide who deftly leads the wine-tasting session I attend, the name of the property was subsequently changed to Denbies to prevent any confusion with the family, which is associated with the pottery industry.

The farmhouse and its grounds were sold to William Wakefield, then to Jonathan Tyers, who bought it as a weekend retreat from London, where he was a skin-trader. Ownership passed through the hands of several others before Denbies was acquired by the Denison banking family then Thomas Cubitt, the top property developer of his day. He was responsible for designing Belgravia and the east façade of Buckingham Palace. Cubitt transformed Denbies into a grand structure, comprising 100 rooms, which was inherited by his son George, a politician who became the first Lord Ashcombe. George was reputedly a kind employer of around 400 townsfolk. However, when he died, the family had to sell off parcels of land to settle the death duties.

During the Second World War, it became the headquarters of the Home Guard – a loyal group of volunteers ineligible for National Service – and was designated a key part of the second line of defence against German attacks in the period that followed the evacuations from the Normandy beaches. Canadian soldiers were based nearby as they prepared to participate in the invasion of France in June 1944. Fortescue's book explains that they left two troop carriers and a tank that were considered unserviceable. The tank was dug up in 1983. It has been restored and now sits in the Tank Museum in Bovington, Dorset.

Meanwhile, Cubitt's grandson demolished the main building and built a smaller one, then reached a deal on the tax debt with the Treasury, which resulted in the ownership of Denbies passing to the National Trust. The Cubitts' dwindling interest finally came to an end in 1984, when Biwater, a water treatment company, bought it on the open market from Harry Cubitt, the fourth Lord Ashcombe.

The Cubitt name is still a feature of the modern Denbies estate and is attached to the most prestigious of the sparkling wines produced here, the Cubitt Blanc de Noirs, which is made from red Pinot Noir grapes. It is seen as a rival to many leading champagnes and is made only when the harvest is deemed to be of a sufficiently high quality.

The man linking Cubitt and the evolution of the wine estate is Adrian White – now Sir Adrian. He was the boss of Biwater, and he snapped up the land and buildings in the 1980s as a head office for his company. At that point, it was a cattle and pig farm. A Dorking resident, Richard Selley, who was a geology professor at Imperial College in London, pointed out the similarities between the land here and in Champagne, suggesting that the chalk soil, south-facing aspect and shelter from the wind made Denbies a perfect site for a vineyard. While this was an interesting and well-researched observation, it was not entirely earth-shattering as land in this part of England has been used intermittently to grow vines since Roman times.

White decided to seize the opportunity and called upon the expertise of the German Viticulture Centres in Trier and Geisenheim for confirmation that winemaking would be viable. Initially, vines from France and Germany were planted on an experimental basis over thirty-five acres of the land, and this was subsequently extended as it became clear which of them grew best in the conditions.

The new owner then broadened out his interests to establish the Denbies Wine Estate, and he set about creating the business, which today accounts for around ten per cent of the vines in the UK. The estate now includes a hotel, restaurants, farm shop, a brewery and workshops that house small businesses including a physio, as well as being a popular place for walkers and runners who avail themselves of the well-signposted paths that traverse the land and offer spectacular views over the Surrey hills when conditions are favourable. A train through the vines is an alternative way for the less energetic to enjoy the scenery.

White's son Chris is chief executive of the business and has provided much of the impetus for its growth. Denbies is now an important employer, with more than 150 staff, having diversified to become an idyllic venue for celebrations such as weddings and other special occasions, as well as producing wine with a burgeoning reputation.

In addition to laying claim to being the biggest vineyard in the UK, Denbies Wine Estate is the venue for my next run. Judging by the daunting slopes that surround its location in the Mole Valley, it is going to offer a stern test of my post-festive season fitness levels.

There's also the matter of the wine, and my chance to make a judgement on which side of the argument I fall – whether the truth is that Denbies is merely leveraged by the hype of English wines and the traditionalists are correct in their criticism, or whether this is home to wines that will play an increasingly important role in the coming years. Or, perhaps, both are correct to some extent.

English wine is often dismissed as having higher prices than those made elsewhere, and therefore offering poorer value. It's a fair argument, but not the full story. One thing

I've discovered while taking a closer look at this is that many vineyards in England are smaller than those elsewhere. What's more, the vines often produce fewer grapes, the techniques are frequently more labour-intensive, and workers may benefit from other factors such as the minimum wage, meaning that overheads are higher.

The winemakers will argue that these factors ensure greater attention throughout each stage and therefore create a better product. I won't get an answer to that debate this afternoon, but I'm hopeful that I will discover something worthy of its place in the case I'm creating when I get to try a few samples.

Denbies produces wines for all tastes, ticking the boxes for lovers of white, red, rosé, orange and, in particular, a bubbly that has garnered great reviews. Fizz now accounts for more than forty per cent of the overall production, with a wide range of quality and prices that matches some of the high-end champagnes from France. Indeed, it is perhaps a sign of the anticipated impact of environmental change that forward-looking French producers are buying up plots of land in England to ensure they are able to continue with their centuries-old traditions should global warming create conditions in northern France that mean that current standards on the other side of the English Channel can't be maintained.

I take the short stroll from Dorking to Denbies, directed by a road sign that points to London and Leatherhead in one direction and simply states 'Vineyard' with an arrow to the left. A long, oak tree-lined drive leads to the buildings, where an art exhibition is taking place and shoppers browse the wines and other goods, possibly killing a few hours ahead of lunch in one of the restaurants. Outside is a hive of activity as dog walkers, joggers and ramblers follow the network of paths. A plaque at the end of one row of vines is a memorial to somebody who clearly enjoyed the open spaces in the latter stages of their life, while lots of people take advantage of the chance to escape the bustle of daily routines and enjoy the solitude or the company of friends in the pastoral surroundings.

I go inside to join a small group and we're welcomed by our tutor. We pick up a glass of bubbly on our way to the cinema to watch a short film, which recounts the history of the property and introduces some of the characters, including Richard Selley, Chris White and the viticulturist Duncan McNeill (together with Clive the Labrador). They explain their respective contributions to the evolution of Denbies.

Duncan talks passionately about the fifteen grape varieties and explains that the standard of the wine that ultimately emerges from those grapes can differ according to where in the vineyard they are planted – the slopes exposed to more variable climatic conditions may produce a product that bears little resemblance to what materialises from more sheltered parts of the vineyard.

It is a great introduction, describing the use of machinery such as the Frostbuster heater and a hot-air fan that is deployed to battle destructive cold weather that can ruin a whole year's harvest if left unchecked. It has replaced more traditional heaters, which provided a prohibitively expensive way of combatting the overnight chill that is a frequent visitor in cooler months.

The film, featuring the music of Vaughan Williams, runs through the seasons, confirming that the task of making good wine is not simply a case of harvesting in autumn then fermenting the grapes. The perilously balanced financial situation is highlighted by the tale of 2012 when frost killed ten per cent of the vines. The first fledgling buds normally appear in May, clusters of fruit emerge in June and weeding takes place in summer, with the weeds mulched to make a form of compost. Vigorous growth in July is followed by what is known as a green harvest in August when unripe berries are culled to reduce the quantity of grapes and enhance the quality.

It falls to the winemaker to make the call on the best timing for the harvest. He is guided by tests that monitor ripeness and help him to decide when sugar and acids are at optimum levels. Typically, it will be late September or early October, with the grapes for red wines normally the last to be picked. Time is of the essence in peak picking season and temporary staff assist with the task of gathering the grapes. The fruit used for the sparkling wine we are drinking as we watch the film is harvested by hand and among the first to be gathered, while other grape varieties will follow over the ensuing weeks. Denbies is the only UK vineyard to have a mechanical picker for the higher-volume grapes. That reduces the lengthy and laborious job of clearing a vine to just four-and-a-half minutes of mechanical effort rather than the many exhausting hours that it would otherwise take. However, it means that the vines must be planted with precision to ensure the machine can pass unhindered without damaging them.

Denbies has stopped using chemical herbicides, which make it possible to keep weeds at bay but can damage organisms that are good for the vines and their roots. That is an early step along the hurdle-strewn road to making wine that meets the exacting requirements to be labelled organic, although this remains a longer-term ambition.

Educated about the background and the attention to detail that defines the wines, we then move on to the tasting. I'm joined by six others in the fermentation room. Along one side are seven barrels depicting the various stages of winemaking. They are carved from oak trees that were destroyed in the 1987 storms and were subsequently sent to an Austrian craftsman who has created ornate carvings on each of the barrels. Tens of thousands of replacement trees have now been planted across the estate. Along an adjacent wall is a rack where sparkling wine undergoes riddling or remuage to collect sediment in the neck of the bottle.

Mona is a knowledgeable and entertaining guide to Denbies wines. She exudes passion for the subject and underlines its importance to her as an accompaniment to food, saying, 'If I can't have a glass of wine with my meal, I'd rather not eat.'

We start with Surrey Gold. This has been in production since 1990 and is the vineyard's best seller. It is pale, almost transparent, and is made using a blend of Müller-Thurgau, Ortega and Bacchus grapes, which are grown on the lower slopes. The taste is fresh and light, and it is easy to imagine having a refreshing glass or two on a warm summer's day. This is a wine that has earned global recognition, having been on the wine lists of UK embassies around the world. The tasting notes suggest it is a good match for a broad range of dishes that seem to have been randomly selected, spicy shredded duck, stir-fried oyster mushrooms and blue cheese tartlets being the examples.

Even lighter is our second wine, Denbies Flint Valley, which is fruitier and has a hint of oak. Like the first one, it is relatively low in alcohol at only eleven per cent, and we're told it is great with fish. We move on to a rosé that is a little darker than many of those made in southern France, and a red that is tasty but not as impressive as the whites we have enjoyed.

There are three winemakers, who have garnered experience in many parts of the winemaking world, and their expertise ensures that Denbies is producing serious wines. The whites are the work of John Worontschak and Matthieu Elzinga, an Australian and a French/Dutchman. In addition to the eclectic talents of that pair, there is another international influence on the final product, with the barrels, bottles and corks all imported. However, that probably shows that the English wine industry is locked into the global network rather than any shortcomings caused by the inability to produce these things locally.

I am impressed by the two whites and opt to add the Surrey Gold to my case, based on it just pipping the Flint Valley because of its place in the history of Denbies. Its price also dispels the myth that English wine is expensive compared with similar styles from elsewhere.

A lunch in the Gallery Restaurant gives me a chance to enjoy the views and has me looking forward to running through the

Denbies vines as the sun continues its job of clearing the frost. It looks idyllic, although I am under no illusions that the hills I can see from my table will definitely offer a challenge when I line up for the run in the morning.

The thing that initially piqued my interest about adding this to my schedule was the fact that there is also an annual wine run for those seeking a fun marathon or a race over half that distance, with wine on offer at the feeding stations alongside the traditional fluids consumed by athletes. Other English vineyards are also now venues for runs, particularly over the summer months. During our tasting, Mona explained that, according to folklore, running through vineyards was an exercise promoted by French winemakers who encouraged their staff to get themselves fit to handle the physical demands of the harvest. Whether that is true or not, I will never know, but the idea has certainly caught on given the extensive Europe-wide list from which I've selected my races.

The idea of covering the full twenty-six miles here in the late summer was an attractive prospect. However, I have other plans for that stage of the year, so I'm here for the Mole Valley parkrun. These runs have become a ritual that has transformed the exercise habits of millions of individuals around the world. Every Saturday, groups line up for a five-kilometre blast that can be as competitive or as social as you like. I suppose I fall somewhere in the middle of those two extremes. I certainly want to perform as well as I can, but I know that I am most likely to feature towards the heart of the bunch, even if things go well.

The parkrun concept started in 2004 when a group of

thirteen runners met up in the London suburb of Teddington. Initial expansion was slow, but gradually it gathered pace. Now more than three million runners get together each Saturday morning at venues around the world for a timed event that is free to participants and always takes place over five kilometres.

Volunteers are an essential part of the occasion, ensuring no one strays off the beaten track and offering help to anyone who suffers an injury. Every participant who carries a bar code receives an email advising them of their result. The founders are adamant that the runs will always be open to everyone – dog walkers and buggy pushers are among the regulars in some of the venues, while others enjoy the camaraderie and the breakfast afterwards more than the physical commitment, but nonetheless turn up week after week to measure their progress.

Running in a group is the motivation many people need to spur them on, and others use parkrun as an introduction to competitive racing or as preparation for other mass-participation events. It has transformed lives, created new friendships and relationships, and is now a fixture in many diaries. It has also created the concept of parkrun tourism, where any runner can turn up at any venue and join the group.

That's exactly what I have done, although the course is a little less beguiling than I had hoped it would be. The scenery was enchantingly wintry when I visited yesterday – the ground was crisp with frost and the air chilled my lungs during my early morning muscle-easing run. The frozen vines glinted in the winter sun, and the vista was glorious. Sadly, that's not the case today. A thick, damp mist hangs heavily in the air and its stubborn refusal to lift thwarts any hope of enjoying the scenery. It is still cold and I'm glad that I chose to dress for comfort rather than style – well-layered and gloved. I certainly wouldn't win any fashions contests, but the muscles should be warm and flexible.

The good news as I jog up towards the venue is that it is cold and fresh. The bad news is that it is not cold enough to freeze the mud, while that obstinate mist is spoiling views of glorious Surrey. A steady stream of cars flows towards the main building and drivers seek a spot in the parking area, which was created specifically to accommodate runners' vehicles.

People of all shapes and sizes feature in the mass of bodies at the start, the younger athletic types elbowing their way to the front, ready to renew personal rivalries from previous weeks, while the social runners gravitate towards the rear, more focused on a jog or a brisk walk and a chat.

This is clearly not a day for setting records. But for the regulars, it is about the conviviality of the occasion and attempting to beat the quickest time they have achieved over this course. That challenge has drawn several hundred runners, all disciples of the parkrun phenomenon. There are no prizes beyond personal satisfaction – whether that is a personal best or simply completing the distance – but it is a fabulous concept that has created many athletes from individuals who would traditionally have spent their Saturday mornings pursuing other activities or, in many cases, would still have been in bed.

Warm-ups involve gentle striding among the vines adjacent

to the start, and groups gather, simultaneously sharing their news and stretching their muscles. Recurring themes for their conversations are the dense fog and the softness underfoot, which was exacerbated by the recent Surrey Cross Country Championships over this course.

Conditions also feature in the pre-run briefing, which delivers information for the benefit of parkrun tourists. The risk of injury as a result of tricky underfoot conditions has been the subject of intense discussions among the volunteers from the local athletics club, but the decision has been made and the run will go ahead, although caution is essential.

'It's not a PB day,' says the announcer with obvious understatement, suggesting that trying to beat personal records should be less important than safely negotiating the course, which, he explains, 'has cut up badly over the past few weeks'. He reads from a well-rehearsed script and mentions the rules and the hazards, including the wires that protrude at the end of the vines, and the risk they present.

Chat completed, the runners are sent on their way, with the first kilometre or so on flat, relatively firm ground marked by cones. That allows the speed merchants to escape off the front and secure the best positions before hitting the first climb of the day.

Typically, that initial ascent would be a decent challenge. Today, it's a brute, the viscous mud an early drain on the energy and a barrier to building any momentum. The paths through the vines are greasy and it pays to seek ways to avoid some of the more glutinous sections. The lack of traction causes me to stall as I approach the top of the climb, and I find it difficult to resume. It's similar to trying to start a car halfway up an icebound hill.

The normally bucolic splendour is still blanketed from view, so there isn't even the compensation of enjoying the picturesque landscape as I skate across the bottomless mud. I see that many of the other runners are wearing trail shoes rather than conventional trainers. Maybe I'm just dredging my shattered ego for an excuse as I question the appropriateness of my footwear – skis or snowshoes would be apposite right now – as this is the second run that has exposed my limited abilities in such testing conditions.

A slither here, and an acceleration there, an uphill slog and an opportunity to stretch the legs on the descent, a short sharp burst to overtake and a feeling of consternation as a pair of perfectly calibrated lungs puff serenely past and disappear into the distance – it's all part of the universal charm of the run.

My struggles are brought into even sharper focus as a yellow-clad figure emerges from the gloom heading towards me. He is a youngster in his early teens who is popping back to check on his mother. She is just behind me and is suffering similar tribulations to those I'm grappling with. He floats effortlessly across the sea of sludge in a manner that suggests he is untroubled by the suction that is sapping my power, or by the slick surface that is proving to be my nemesis.

I briefly manage to stride out but soon hit another hazard. The fact that I am now running across the hill means that my inadequate technique steers me left and I slide towards the vines. My natural style is to run on top of the ground rather than plod through cloying mud, but that is simply impossible in these conditions, and it is a relief when the next change of direction is a right turn and another climb.

I slither around the bend then negotiate a short flat section before the path bends to the left for the first downhill section. To revisit the car analogy, I am now freewheeling, as any effort to control my pace is futile.

And then, at last, we hit solid ground and there is a chance to raise the pace without risk of injury. I glance at my watch and see that I'm finally going at a decent pace. That proves short-lived and we cross a concrete path then return to the quagmire. Again, we are running across the hill and I am unable to fight the gravitational pull. I manage to overtake a couple of runners and I am closing the gap on two immediately ahead of me, trying to emulate their steps as they negotiate their way around the deepest puddles.

I move to the dryer ground to the right of the path, but have forgotten the warning we were given at the start. I am making progress when my foot hits a wire inserted at the end of a row of vines. I tumble and quickly bounce back to my feet. The yellow-clad youngster sails past while one of the others I just overtook checks that I am not injured and offers his assessment – 'nice roll!'

It takes me a couple of moments to raise the pace to its former level, and I progress steadily until we complete the fourth kilometre and I recognise where we are. A right turn means we are descending what was the initial climb. This should be when I muster a sprint but I'm unable to make up ground on the two runners ahead of me. One daredevil has released the mental handbrake and comes thundering past in kamikaze fashion, although he is forced wide when it comes to the final right turn onto the firmer grassy surface that is solid enough to allow me to finish with a flourish.

I will learn when the results arrive later that, incredibly, several runners have managed to clock a personal best, although only two have dipped below twenty minutes, evidence of the testing nature of the circuit. Each parkrun measures the same distance, but as today's experience shows, that is not the only factor when it comes to the final clocking. This route bears very little similarity to the pancake-flat waterfront lap that makes the Edinburgh run where I usually take part one of the fastest in the country. Indeed, my effort to negotiate the Denbies vines will prove to be more than five minutes slower than the best I've achieved on my home course. If I'm clutching at straws, I will take some solace from the fact that I am fourth quickest in my age category, but in truth I'm disappointed with the way it has gone.

However, there's no time to dwell on that. Many parkrun participants follow a post-run habit of a revitalising coffee and, here, they enjoy a discount in the vineyard café if they produce their barcode. That's not on my agenda today as I must now go back to the hotel to shower and change before heading into London to report on a rugby match.

I jog back, my feet still wet and my trainers heavy with mud. As I approach the hotel it occurs to me that I won't be able to enter without leaving a trail of chalky clay, something which will not endear me to the staff. I take my shoes off in the car park and bang them together, sending mud in all directions. The manager expresses his gratitude as I pass the reception in my stocking soles, although the remnants mean I will have a little bit of England's largest vineyard in my luggage when I travel home tomorrow.

It has been an interesting introduction to English wine and I can see why its reputation is growing. Denbies is at the forefront of a trend that should continue to evolve and gather pace. I'm hoping that I can do the same.

Glass half-full moment: The fabulous parkrun atmosphere and an introduction to English wine

Glass half-empty moment: Not being able to enjoy the spectacular scenery

Wine selected for Colin's Case: Surrey Gold

Five

GERMANY

TUNE OF THE DAY:
'Cold as Ice' – Foreigner

'The best laid schemes o' mice an' men gang aft agley', as Burns said in his poem 'To a Mouse'. And, here, a couple of weeks after the life of Scotland's bard was celebrated around the world, is proof that being organised well in advance comes with no guarantee that an idea will reach fruition.

My intention had been to run an underground ten kilometre race in Moldova. The event was due to celebrate the contribution Europe's poorest country has made to the world of wine. Viticulture has been a part of its landscape for many centuries, with archaeologists having uncovered signs of winemaking dating back to the tenth millennium BC, while a local priest found documents from the fifteenth century lurking in a dark corner of his church.

That storied past goes some way towards explaining how the Mileştii Mici winery accumulated a collection of more than a million and a half bottles in cellars that are recognised as the largest anywhere on the globe, covering around 200 kilometres and sitting at a depth of eighty-five metres. That ensures the wine is stored at the ideal temperature and means it is always in excellent condition.

It's where Vladmir Putin kept his personal wine collection, apparently, and the cellars have links to British royalty through King George V and Queen Victoria, who were both fans of Moldovan produce. So, too, was Hermann Göring, whose hoard, gathered from countries occupied by Germany during the Second World War, was subsequently taken to Moscow and much of it drunk by Soviet soldiers.

It all sounded amazing and, excited by the prospect of running through tunnels, this was the first run I entered when I started to finalise my race programme. However, communication was sparse and when I did finally hear from the organisers it was to tell me that the event was cancelled. There was no real explanation. Sadly, I'll have to leave my investigation for another day.

That message, which I eventually received after much chasing, prompted me to find a late replacement for the February slot on my schedule.

Step forward a worthy substitute. Germany and I have history. Until my trip to Switzerland last October, it was the only country outside the UK where I had donned my running shoes. That was back in my final year at school when I spent three months as the guest of a welcoming family in the little Bavarian town of Rehau – located at the time on the tip of a triple border between East Germany, West Germany and Czechoslovakia. That frontier disappeared a while ago, but my memories of a divided nation remain vivid.

I recall that I was left in the capable hands of neighbours one weekend because my hosts were venturing to the other side of the Iron Curtain. Close relatives, who lived just a couple of miles away, were now in the East after the border was constructed without warning, creating a barrier that separated family members, and meant visits were rare, as well as being bound in red tape. This reunion had been many months in the planning, and I wasn't able to join them for the trip. It's one of the many recollections etched on my memory of a geopolitical situation I found absorbing, but did not fully understand.

There were occasions when I would lie in bed wondering whether the barking of dogs that I could hear was a sign that fugitives seeking to escape from the communist East had been captured, or merely a warning that any attempt to flee would be pointless.

Unnerving though it was for a callow teenager who had led a sheltered life in the Scottish Borders, I soon became accustomed to the nightly intrusion. Overall, my German foray was hugely positive. My social development and language skills benefited greatly from the experience of attending school, although it didn't do much for my maths, which was already poor in my native tongue and nigh on impossible in translated form.

Germany is a beautiful country populated by people who are generally much kinder and more open than they are given credit for. Subsequent visits have reaffirmed the many positive features of a nation that is often maligned by those whose judgement of its people is defined by feuds over sun loungers secured by the deft use of towels while on a Balearic Island holiday.

I have another souvenir of my German experience – a certificate that was my reward for third place in a cross-country race in the town of Wunsiedel, together with a newspaper cutting that records my performance (an online search while preparing for this trip reveals that the winner is still competing). That result earned me a little kudos from my hosts. It also confirmed the value of my training runs along the base of the daunting boundary fence under the watchful gaze of armed border guards who would follow my progress intently from their lookout posts, although clearly I was no putative escapee, being on the western side.

I recall that my host and I spent school holidays cycling around the southern part of the country, staying in youth hostels. Many of them were what might euphemistically be described as 'off the beaten track'. Those adventures revealed to me that Germany is dotted with towns and villages that ooze chocolate-box quaintness.

That is a striking characteristic of much of Esslingen, a university town near Stuttgart in Baden-Württemberg with a population just shy of 100,000, although even the official website seems unsure whether it is a town or a city. The University of Applied Sciences has three campuses and almost 6,500 students, many of them from other countries. That young population plays its part in the vibrant mood that pervades the cafés and restaurants. The sight of students brings to memory another aspect of my German school experience. I recall the tension at the start of each day when we would go into classes and there was an element of foreboding. It soon became clear that the reason for that nervousness was the practice of teachers picking on students and testing their knowledge – the dreaded extemporal live exam, or 'ex' to the students. This entailed one individual being called to the front of the class where they would be grilled by the teacher on various matters covered so far during the term. The result had a bearing on the final mark for the year. Being chosen was stressful, and many students would crumble, while others would relish the pressure. I wonder whether that practice is still a feature of the school system from which the current generation of young people has recently emerged, and if the experience proved to be positive or damaging for my classmates.

Another local characteristic in Esslingen is that around five per cent of the people are Turkish, evidence, I assume, of how reliant the area was on immigration in the 1960s. The immigrant imprint perhaps explains why I hear many inter-generational conversations being conducted in what I take to be Turkish. That background is also reflected in the diverse culture, with a large number of kebab shops sitting next to long-established German bakeries as a source of takeaway food that is often eaten in the streets as people go about their daily business. In addition, many Italians, Greeks and Croats have settled here, perhaps drawn by the easy availability of work over the years. It's interesting to see several pages of job adverts in the local paper, the *Eßlinger Zeitung*. That's a rarity in British media these days.

Another aspect of the landscape that strikes me as unusual is the existence in the main shopping area of an old-school tobacconist and two hat shops. Though seemingly unfashionable, they clearly do enough trade to stay in business.

The cobbled medieval centre features Gothic churches whose towering presence is enhanced by original stained-glass features, and where the silence is broken by the hum of tourist voices and bells that chime at set times each day. Signs above shops are often hand-painted onto the buildings in traditional style, adding to the feeling of antiquity.

A few steps away from the main streets sit residential areas that appear to have lain unchanged for several centuries, and only the high-value cars offer a hint that this is a prosperous modern place to live.

Adding to the feeling of history and tradition are the two town halls. The original one was completed in 1423 and used as a place for commerce and tax collection. The newer building was a private home for the influential Palm family, who were distinguished bankers and diplomats. Built in 1763, it became the new town hall in 1841.

Nestled in the narrow lane leading off the main square is a building that is among Germany's oldest half-timbered houses, dating back to around 1330. In the other direction is the centre, and as I head that way, my attention is grabbed by the sight of the Skywalker statue, a sculpture created in the 1980s and emerging from the thirteenth-century Schelztor Gate Tower, which was originally part of the town's fortifications. The artwork depicts a man balanced precariously on a thin steel girder. It could prove disconcerting for anyone gazing skywards after a few glasses of the local wine.

The Neckar river flows serenely by and at one point blends with the Rossneckar and Wehrneckar tributaries in a part of town known as Little Venice. Esslingen Castle sits proudly above the city, surrounded by the vines that offer a clue as to why this run is on my list, although the grapes are not used for the sparkling wine that has made this place famous. Nor are the miles of others that sprawl across the slopes heading out of town. They will largely be used to create some of the region's still wines.

Baden-Württemberg is among Germany's more prosperous states. It is particularly well-known for its contribution to the auto industry. On the 122 bus into Esslingen, as we pass villages with multi-syllabic names, it's noticeable that there is some German car chauvinism going on here. That's not really surprising when the local possibilities are so numerous. Mercedes, Audi and VW vie for a place on the popularity podium, while an occasional boy-racer speeds past ostentatiously in a top-of-the-range Porsche. Stuttgart boasts dedicated museums for Mercedes-Benz and Porsche among its tourist attractions.

Esslingen features on the Württemberger Weinstrasse, a popular tourist route of more than 500 kilometres through the region's wine-growing areas. The town's vinification tradition is equally well-established. It plays its part in creating a good range of still wines and the path up to the castle features several patches of familiar grape varieties, as well as stories of the people who transform them. But Esslingen is best known for its role in producing Sekt, a German sparkling wine. That is thanks to the efforts of Georg Christian von Kessler, who remains synonymous with top-notch bubbly and whose name is sprinkled around the centre, in street names, signs that adorn the winery where the product is made, the bar where it is sold and in the town's museum.

His is a tale of optimistic enterprise melded with sadness. The young Georg studied business and lived for a while in Reims, the capital of the Champagne region in France, where he worked as an accountant for Veuve Clicquot, rising to the position of partner in the company. The official story suggests that he left France for his native Germany when he was foiled in his bid to secure the chief executive's job. A more scurrilous version posits the notion that his relationship with the widow Clicquot was a little more than a business arrangement and that this was what prompted his departure.

Regardless of which is closer to the truth – both may be accurate to some extent – he returned to Esslingen in 1826. Tucked away in his memory bank was the secret of secondary fermentation techniques – adding sugar and yeast to create carbon dioxide – that ensured consistency and excellence in champagne production, as well as a marketeer's insight into how best to succeed in selling sparkling wine to his own townsfolk.

Kessler used that knowledge to build a business that continues to operate from a traditional building, constructed in the early thirteenth century, close to the Stadtkirche and located in the square that now bears his name. This was formerly a monastery where local tax was collected, but its purpose changed when Kessler acquired it as a base. Below the building sit two kilometres of tunnels housing twelve linked cellars where the wine is made and visitors can sample the end result.

I resist that temptation for now as I have a run on my agenda. It's another parkrun, showing how the network of events is gradually extending its positive reach to new audiences. This one was added to the global schedule of five-kilometre events in 2019. And while the number of participants is smaller than the run I'm accustomed to in Edinburgh, its popularity is growing and past results show that it has attracted some talented athletes. The course records are held by the Kenyan stars Ernest Kibet Tarus and Grace Kwamboka Momanyi who, I will later learn, used the run as a bit of fun training during the build-up to their wins at the Ljubljana International Marathon in Slovenia. Their times suggest that top athletes can cover the course swiftly, although runners of such calibre would probably expect to go faster than they achieved. So, unless they were holding back, there's maybe something about the run that is more challenging than a mere face-value assessment would attest.

Some other German races jostled for a place on my schedule, but the advantage of this one is that, as the parkrun takes place every Saturday, I can slot it into any available space. That has proved its worth in this instance following the Moldova cancellation. The proper title of the Esslingen event is the Neckarufer parkrun, in recognition of the fact that it follows the riverbank for much of the way.

I arrive in time to join in the pre-run chat and I'm joined at the start by a small but intriguingly diverse group of runners and volunteers, including Chris, who falls into both camps.

He is an ex-pat bundle of energy, who moved from East Sussex and has lived here for more than two decades. Chris is the parkrun representative for Germany, having initially launched a run in Stuttgart before setting up this one. He addresses a handful of first-time runners in German then recaps in English for my benefit.

I had a little recce yesterday and discovered that there are some narrow parts as well as a couple of tight bends. While it is generally flat, there are one or two small hills, although nothing that could be described as a tough climb.

The narrow sections on the riverside path could make it tricky if there were large numbers of runners, particularly as it is a public space shared with cyclists, dog walkers and, as I'll find out, anglers. The record entry was more than 100, but today's line-up numbers only twenty-eight, so congestion is unlikely to be an issue.

There's still a risk of some slippery sections given the temperature is a brisk minus two, but thankfully the snow that was forecast has failed to materialise and the thick mist hanging over the Neckar is starting to lift, offering a tantalising glimpse of some sunshine.

There's admirable keenness among the volunteers, who will ensure safety is paramount, mark the turns on the course and record the times. An enthusiastic countdown sends us on our way, and immediately it's clear that the duo at the front are battling to finish first. That contest will eventually be won by Sebastian who is several minutes quicker than everyone else.

They disappear into the distance and I settle into a stride that is comfortable. Chris has swapped his organiser's hat for his other role as runner and is ahead of me. He's a useful athlete, as shown by his personal best. He made sure he was fully warmed up by covering the seven-and-a-half kilometres from home this morning and is running well with an economical stride that propels him easily.

Chris looks round and spots me then kindly drops back to chat. He asks about my trip and explains a little about his role in setting up parkrun Germany. Our conversation helps the first kilometre to pass at a reasonable pace and prevent me from falling into the trap of going too fast in the early stages.

The initial part is generally flat followed by a tiny climb before we reach a point where a helper directs us to round a plastic cone and we head back towards the start, meaning the Neckar is now on our left. My watch beeps with a note of my pace for the first mile – I'm still an imperial measures man – and I appear to be ticking along relatively comfortably.

Chris clearly wants to press on a little, so I urge him to do so, and he quickly leaves me in his wake, covering the remaining distance at an impressively quick pace to finish with a good time. Now running on my own, my stride falters slightly. I hear breathing approach from behind and I'm overtaken by a runner who turns out to be Kitty, a regular on this course. She goes past me and opens a slight gap, but I remain in her slipstream. That's handy because, although arrows chalked on the side of the path show the direction we should be following, there is an unlikely twist around the two-kilometre mark with a sharp left turn through a doorway and across a small wooden bridge. This is part of the Water House, which sits next to a dam on the river. The building has been around since the early nineteenth century and remains in use today. Running through doorways at either end of the bridge, which is shaded by the house roof, feels a little like intruding on private property. It also forces another slight easing of the pace at which I'm travelling. Perhaps it also explains why top Kenyan internationals did not post world-class times when they were setting the course records.

We emerge back onto the path, which curves to the right, forcing us to slow down again, although a slight downhill helps me to accelerate a little. Ahead is a straight stretch, which is the ideal place to extend my stride. However, two anglers are setting up for a day of fishing and are laying out their equipment. Fortunately, they see Kitty approaching and take evasive action, which also allows me to pass unhindered.

We meet the leaders coming in the opposite direction and pass through the third kilometre, a milestone that is illustrated by a message that has been chalked in the middle of the path by a volunteer and is annotated with a promise that the sun is coming out soon. My mental calculations tell me that we must be reaching the turning point, and that proves to be the case as we perform another 180-degree manoeuvre before heading for home.

We re-cross the wooden bridge at the Water House and, although my second mile is a little slower than the first, I'm feeling reasonably good. I close the gap on Kitty and, just after completing the fourth kilometre, I overtake her, although she digs in and I'll find out later that she has recorded a personal best. I pass the skateboard park that signals the start of the home straight and I finish strongly, although the course has one last test in store, a short sharp climb to the yellow Ziel sign that marks the finish.

Lars, another among the gang of helpers, congratulates me by name and scans my bar code to ensure I'm given an official time. It's not my quickest parkrun, but I finish comfortably in the top ten and I'm quickest in the old man's category. I convince myself that the idiosyncrasies of the course are worth enough seconds to make it a decent performance relative to what I've achieved on my home patch in Edinburgh. The day's biggest cheer is for one runner who ends with a flourish to complete his comeback from a recent heart attack.

The camaraderie continues as several in the group head for breakfast at a café on the other side of the river. Meanwhile, Chris sets off on his return journey, adding a few more kilometres to his weekly tally.

It has been a fun morning with a great bunch of people, and a perfect way to set up the rest of my day, which starts with a run back to the hotel for a shower and a refuel before heading off to learn a little more about Herr Kessler and his wine.

My accommodation is handy for the run, being a good warm-up jog away, but is a little way from the Old Town. Another factor in my choice of hotel was its green credentials, which include the widespread use of natural materials and energy-efficient lightbulbs, plus the absence of plastics. Business practices throughout the town lean towards behaviour that is environmentally friendly, and one of the busiest corners of where I'm staying is a machine that accepts glass and plastic bottles and offers cash to those who hand back their empties. I seem to remember that being a feature of my life in Scotland fifty years ago, although no machines were involved at that time – progress indeed.

I've booked a spot on a tasting and when I reach the centre of town it is buzzing. A market in the square is doing lively business and an earlier tour has spilled onto the street in front of the winery, with the group noisily topping up glasses from bottles they have bought in the shop, or at the adjoining bar.

Our gathering of twenty meets outside the heavy, ornately carved wooden door. It swings open and our guide steps outside. She introduces herself, as Sandra I think, although a cork popping in the background means it's not entirely clear. She invites us to come inside and we climb the creaking wooden staircase to sign in and pay. As there are too few visitors to justify an English-speaking guide, the tour is conducted in German, so it's a good test of my language skills.

Our guide leads us to the first cellar and explains that this was where Kessler suffered his first major setback as a winemaker. While in France, he had discovered the importance of a heavier bottle in withstanding the explosive combination of yeast and sugar. That proved to be an issue when he returned to Germany. Our guide tells us that in his first year many of the bottles shattered during fermentation. It was an expensive lesson as around half of the wine was lost, leaving him only 4,000 bottles, which were modestly called *Sparkling Wine from Württemberg*, although he did mention on the label that he had previously worked with Veuve Clicquot, something that would enhance the attractiveness of his product to those in the know.

Eventually, Kessler found a German glassmaker who could emulate what he had seen in France, and the problem was solved. Within a decade he had sold around half a million bottles and exported much of what he produced to Russia, the UK and America, as well as seeing significant demand from his home market, including the country's royalty. The year 1826 is now embossed on all Kessler Sekt bottles.

Kessler owned a vineyard in his home town of Heilbronn, but didn't trust the quality of the grapes and looked beyond Germany's borders to find suitable supplies. He relied on his winemaking skills to ensure the final product was of a high enough standard for his name to appear on the eight-cornered label that he had also copied from his former employer in Reims. Nowadays, the grapes come from elsewhere in Germany and from Italy before being crafted into a high-end product by staff in Esslingen.

Labels have always been a big deal. At one stage, the company employed a celebrated cartoonist to design an image, which appeared on some of Kessler's bottles. This depicts two waiters – known in the hospitality industry as Piccolos – carrying an ice bucket containing a bottle of Kessler Sekt. This is now the company logo, while Piccolo is the name given to the 200-millilitre bottle that is popular among customers. However, despite evolving and changing colour, the label's shape remains loyal to the original eight-cornered form and is viewed as an iconic element of the Kessler brand.

A screen is lowered from the ceiling and we are shown a film that features the company's sommelier and the cellar master, who explain a little more about the methods they use. As with the stages that go into champagne making, Sekt matures in bottles. They are stored in a rack as they mature and are turned by hand to ensure the yeast settles in the neck, forming a stopper. The film shows that the steps towards removing the stopper mirror what happens in champagne production – the bottle neck is plunged into ice, the lid is removed and the resulting lump is removed by a machine before the contents are topped up using still wine, and the maturing continues.

The origins of the name Sekt are unclear. One version of the history behind it states that Shakespeare inadvertently played a part. The character Falstaff, who appears in *Henry IV*, has a line in which he orders a Portuguese wine, saying, 'Give me a cup of sack, boy.' This is said to have prompted Ludwig Devrient, a German actor, to use the phrase in a Berlin wine bar in 1825. The waiter mistakenly assumed Devrient was referring to champagne and the word Sekt became a slang word for sparkling wine in Berlin.

Kessler's business proved successful, but his personal life was less so, and he tragically lost both his wife and son to illnesses. That left him with no one to inherit the business, so on his death it passed to his best friend, Carl Weiss. At the time of that handover in 1842, there were annual sales of around 46,000 bottles and the success continued under Weiss. Subsequent generations also drove expansion.

The company's history tells the story of the war years, when male employees were conscripted to the army and the roles at the winery were filled by workers from Eastern Europe, many of whom subsequently stayed on.

An important development came in 1956, when Chancellor

Konrad Adenauer visited the cellars. He was known as a wine connoisseur, and he decided that official visitors to Germany should be offered the Kessler Hochgewächs, which was dubbed 'Chancellor Sekt' as a result. Other heads of state who are known to have shared Adenauer's appreciation include Charles de Gaulle and John F. Kennedy. Kessler Hochgewächs was also served on the world voyage of the Graf Zeppelin airship.

Sales topped a million bottles in 1969 but difficulties lay ahead and the company had to be bailed out in 2005 by a consortium of investors. Since then, Kessler has managed to survive and thrive, with new sales avenues opening up and the company building on its reputation as Germany's oldest and most traditional sparkling wine maker. That has involved creating additional products and finding new markets.

These days, around 400 million bottles of bubbly are consumed in Germany, according to data from the Federal Statistical Office. That makes the Germans the world leaders, out-slurping Brits, Americans and even the French. The high levels of demand have driven many small winemaking businesses to branch out into Sekt over recent years. It strikes me, given the rate at which I have seen it being drunk in Esslingen at all hours of the day, a new record is likely before too long.

Sandra leads the group into a wood-panelled room adorned with pictures of the men who drove the company's success, hung alongside ornate etchings. We will be tasting three wines. She starts with the Hochgewächs, which is still made following the original method, using Chardonnay grapes.

She tells us that the smaller the bubbles in the glass, the better the wine. She also explains that, in addition to attracting the support of Adenauer, this one was the choice of the Hollywood actor Errol Flynn, whose visit to the cellar is recalled in a photo gallery on the wall of the chic wine bar next door. With a cheery 'zum Wohl', she drinks to our health and the tasters return the compliment.

Our glasses are refilled with a vintage rosé, which is rich with flavour, unlike much of the pink sparkling wine I've tasted in the past. This was added to the product range by the new owners who are looking to broaden out the customer base without deviating too much from tradition.

We finish off with a taste of one of the older products, the Jägergrün, which is a little dryer than the others and is made from Riesling, Germany's main white grape variety, and has been sold by Kessler for more than a century. Among our group is a bunch of four lads, one of whom is accompanied by his girlfriend. Their boisterous behaviour leads me to suspect that the tasting is not their first brush with alcohol today, and that notion is underlined when Sandra pours our third sample. The girlfriend waves her glass and points out that 'there is still some room'. Sandra obliges, filling it to the brim.

We move to the shop, where I will buy the next of my twelve wines. I've enjoyed each of the three, but my decision is guided by the history attached to the Hochgewächs, so that's the one that finds its way into my case.

Others in our group are buying bottles and glasses, which I suspect will be put to immediate use as we emerge into the weak winter sun.

Sunday offers a chance to enjoy Esslingen's deserted streets before I leave. The town is slowly emerging from its slumber, with the silence broken by an occasional passing car or the peal of a church bell. As is the case in many European countries, the shops and many of the bars and restaurants remain closed, while those that are open attract a steady flow of early-morning strollers. It's a peaceful and very comfortable environment.

As I wait for the 122 bus back to Stuttgart, I reflect on my long weekend. Germany has been as fascinating as ever. A few days is never long enough to get a handle on the people of a foreign country. I had a bit of a head start in this case, and I leave with my own prejudices and judgements reaffirmed. There's no doubt that some Germans take life very seriously. But it's equally clear to me that many are good fun, and a good number also have a carefree approach that is often underestimated.

This wasn't the run I had planned for this month, nor was it the event I had pencilled in for Germany. But that simply underlines the need to be adaptable in my arrangements. I'm pleased to have chosen Esslingen as my stand-by. It is a lovely place to spend a few days, while the run was relaxed and friendly. I certainly wouldn't rule out a return trip at some point in the future.

As had been the case the previous month, the run played second fiddle to the wine-tasting aspect of my trip. That's about to change as things click up a gear for the next race on my list.

Glass half-full moment: A good wine-tasting and a warm welcome from the parkrunners

Glass half-empty moment: Being disappointed at the cancellation of the underground run in Moldova

Wine selected for Colin's Case: Kessler Hochgewächs

Six

SPAIN

TUNE OF THE DAY:
'Sherry Baby' – Frankie Valli

I've always been aware that the biggest risk to successfully completing this twelve-run adventure is a possible breakdown in the health and fitness of a sixty-year-old man. Sadly, I was forced to abandon plans for a race and a wine run in Cyprus in March. That has caused a reshuffle and I'm now looking to fill the gap that disappointing turn of events has left in my schedule. However, finding a replacement can wait for now.

I'm now almost back to what passes as fully fit these days, although a persistent niggle in my Achilles means there is still a risk each time I pull on my running shoes. I'm relishing this trip for many reasons. On this occasion, I have company. I'm travelling with my son, Lewis. He's an accomplished athlete, a talented triathlete, and great fun to be with. Lewis is a handy man to have with me, as he's a fluent Spanish speaker, with a first-class honours degree from Glasgow University as proof. During his studies, he spent a year living in Spain, and his interest in the country means he's knowledgeable about its history. One other thing that makes him the ideal companion for this trip is that he works in the wine industry.

Lewis is currently training for an ironman triathlon, but has agreed to plod round the vineyards of Jerez de la Frontera at my pace rather than chase a high placing in the overall standings. It's a rare window in his busy timetable, so I want to enjoy a few days with him.

For most people of my generation, sherry has a bit of an image problem. It comes with a memory of many a New Year's Day when families would come together to celebrate fresh hope for a prosperous future. The bottle – probably QC or Emva Cream (although other equally unfathomable names were available) – would be lurking at the rear of granny's drinks cabinet alongside the advocaat, another anachronism that is still available but has fallen from the prominence it once enjoyed. She would fish the bottle out, blow off the cobwebs, pour a small glass for each guest and return the sherry to its resting place where it would languish for another twelve months before that routine was repeated.

Of course, a year later, its condition would have deteriorated even more. No one seemed to acknowledge that this beverage that appeared only for special occasions was wine and should be treated in the same way as that bottle of Black Tower or Piat d'Or – also icons of the era – and consumed over a short period, no more than a few months at the very most if it was of good quality. If only granny had known that. Apparently, one thing she did get right was her decision to store the bottle in a standing position.

Thankfully those times are now gone, and greater wine

sophistication has led to us seeing sherry for the versatile drink it is. Producers have also learned to market their product more effectively and, although the six styles remain a mystery to many, an increasing number of Britons now know that fino is the lightest in colour and most straightforward, while the darkest is oloroso, which is aged longer than the others and, consequently, has a more concentrated flavour.

I look forward to trying to discern the differences while I'm here for the more serious task of running the half-marathon. We've arrived in Andalucia at a stage of the year when the mercury is starting to nudge a little higher, although, as the dense greenery of the landscape suggests, rain is a frequent visitor during the spring.

Ahead of my trip, I had assumed that even in late April, with the peak summer heat still some way off, chestnut-brown locals would languish in the cool shadows cast by the ubiquitous citrus trees, sitting contentedly in picturesque squares dotted with fountains, and streets seemingly littered with a surfeit of architecturally stunning churches and palaces.

That romantic image is dispelled as we arrive in a heavy shower, the first of many that are forecast for the next couple of days, although the weather will be mercifully benign, both in terms of rainfall and temperatures, for our run on Sunday.

Jerez de la Frontera sits around twelve miles from the Atlantic coast and lives in the shadow of its larger neighbours, Seville and Cadiz. However, its stunning Moorish architecture and status as the global sherry capital make this an alluring place to visit. It is twinned with various cities around the world that have a connection with alcohol, including Bristol

– which has strong links to sherry – Tequila in Mexico, Pisco in Peru and the French town of Cognac.

It has a population around 215,000, placing it just outside Spain's twenty largest cities, and combines a colourful past with a vibrant present. I've read that the average age of its citizens – Jerezanos, as they're known – is forty-five, and there are around seventy people who are older than 100.

The city's tradition is built on several institutions. One of the most renowned is the Royal Andalusian School of Equestrian Art, a prestigious establishment with a reputation that spreads around the globe. Another non-negotiable part of the local culture is flamenco. The city is often described as home to this folkloric art form, although there are counterclaims by both Seville and Cadiz. A major flamenco festival takes place in the city each year, attracting visitors from around the world to enjoy emotion-rich performances that are intense and transfixing. It's a combination of sounds and movement and something that intrigues and enthrals anyone who witnesses it. I'm hoping to see it live, although I'm unsure whether I'll be able to interpret the meaning or intricacy of the movement. I suppose that's to be expected of someone whose dancing days peaked at the school leavers' ball in 1979.

Among the more modern features is Circuito de Jerez – also known as the Angel Nieto race track – which previously hosted the Spanish Formula One Grand Prix, but is best known as a venue for superbike racing. Motorbike heroes are given the Hollywood treatment in Jerez, with a pavement walk of fame where decorative stars embedded in the pavement pay tribute to some of the sport's biggest names.

Meanwhile, drawing on both ancient and modern is the process of making sherry. To carry the name, it must come from the area referred to as Marco de Jerez, or the Sherry Triangle. Three towns are responsible for its production – Jerez de la Frontera, Sanlúcar de Barrameda and El Puerto de Santa Maria.

Every bar, café and restaurant serves several styles of the regional speciality at prices that make it cheaper than any soft-drink alternative. While some people may stop for a chilled fino while out strolling, it's as an accompaniment to food in the tapas bars, or tabancos as they're known, that it is more widely consumed. Many of those places have been around for decades or more, and are venues for flamenco, as well as a place to eat, something that is high on our list of essentials a few hours after arriving.

The oldest in the city is the Tabanco El Pasaje, which has existed for almost a century. Lewis and I head off to investigate. We manage to squeeze into this L-shaped space shortly before the start of the regular flamenco show. The exposed brick walls are decorated with posters telling of bullfights and sherry-making, and tables are at a premium. We find a place to sit and Lewis goes to the bar to order some food, together with a glass of amontillado, the second-driest of the sherry types and distinguished from fino by its slightly darker colour, which is a result of it having been exposed to oxygen during the winemaking process. Our tapas arrive on greaseproof paper rather than plates and our order is noted on a chalkboard at the bar. The audience is largely Spanish, a welcome sign that, despite its reputation, El Pasaje is not a tourist trap. The flamenco takes place in a corner that we can only see via the mirror above the bar, but we hear the increasingly frenzied guitar-strumming and the wailing that is an integral part of the tradition. I don't think I'll ever become a huge follower, but it drips with emotion and is mesmerising. We decide to move on and go to pay the bill. The barman tallies up the numbers on the chalkboard – no chance of a receipt here – and we settle up.

Streets, which were deserted a few hours ago during the afternoon siesta, now teem with people and we join the evening strollers for a first sight of this city where religion and sherry-making sit shoulder to shoulder in the cultural history. There are around forty churches and religious organisations, each occupying buildings created by what must have been years of painstaking effort. In addition to enjoying the loyalty of people who remain committed to their faith, they are home to some ornate sculptures and artworks.

We have arrived in Jerez as the Semana Santa celebrations are reaching an end. This translates as Holy Week, and commemorates the Passion of Christ. While we're here, we'll see various examples of the religious commitment of the citizens, including one occasion when a crowd of solemn worshippers enters the Convento de Santo Domingo by the main entrance then exits at the side, having gathered a few more followers, and sets off on a procession led by the priest and with a silver band bringing up the rear.

Work is underway to dismantle street-side grandstands, which have been erected around the city to allow spectators to celebrate the events, and regional television provides extensive coverage, including the views of what appear to be a couple of pundits. It's also the subject of a double-page spread in the local newspaper, *Diario de Jerez*.

The weighty influence of the church is not the only tradition that remains intact. The city's bullring is also a focus for an activity that still enjoys the support of many Spaniards, despite growing opposition elsewhere in the world. It's a sign of the passionate support for the activity that bullfighting garners one page of the paper and includes a picture of two picadors – one type of exponent – being paraded on the shoulders of fans. That's the same as the space allocated to the Spanish Cup victory of local football side Real Betis over Valencia.

Streets near the bullring bear names such as Juan Antonio Romero and Juan Belmonte to prove the hero status of matadors. Meanwhile, the arena's external walls show the names of famous bulls, together with those who brought them down. While there's nothing happening today, it's clear that bullfighting is still an activity driven by class, with tickets in the shade costing more than those in the blazing sun, which is where the less well-off spectators will be seated.

While the old town is a warren of narrow cobbled streets, a short walk away is the main road into the centre. It is lined by orange trees whose branches groan with over-ripe fruit, which is a hazard for pedestrians as it falls and splatters across the ground.

In the heart of the town is the picturesque Plaza Arenal. Its focal point is a statue of Miguel Primo de Rivera, a native of Jerez, who became dictator of Spain in the 1920s. He led a military coup and imposed martial law. However, Miguel apparently enjoyed the good life. He would often make political decisions while under the influence, and would be forced to rescind them when sobriety struck the following day. He resigned in 1930 and was followed by his son, who formed the Falange Party from which Franco emerged. There's a hint of irony that the buildings that overlook this fountain-fringed memorial to a dictator include the headquarters of the libertarian socialist CGT workers union.

The local wineries, or bodegas as they're known, are dotted across the city. Varying in size and speciality, some are more visit-worthy than others. Among those on my shortlist are Tio Pepe, the world's largest sherry producer, and Fundacion, which makes high quality sherry as well as boasting a collection of works by artists including Goya, El Greco and Velasquez. And there's Fundador, which claims to be the oldest, having been involved in making sherry since 1730.

We choose the third of these as the place where we will seek to quench our thirst for knowledge about sherry. Our guide is a well-versed, enthusiastic ambassador for the brand. We are part of a twenty-strong group that starts our tour in one of Fundador's three wineries. Here, in the sprawling building, is a glimpse of the magnitude of this business. Everything is designed to maximise the standard of the final product, from the height of the windows as a means of regulating the amount of light that enters, to the barrels, which are handmade on site from American oak to ensure they are perfectly suited for the job.

The significance of the number three is a recurring theme in the commentary. There's the trio of places in the Sherry

Triangle, the grapes that are used – Palomino, Moscatel and Pedro Ximenez – and the fact that all sherry is at least three years old. It is made using the Solera system. This involves three barrels piled high and is designed to ensure consistency.

The youngest wine sits on top of the others, the middle barrel contains sherry aged up to three years, and the one on the bottom is at least ten years old. Each year one-third of the contents will be removed from the bottom barrel and sent for bottling. A similar amount will be removed from the middle barrel and used to fill the gap and it, in turn, will be replenished using the contents of the top barrel, where new wine will be added to ensure all three barrels are full.

The consequence of mixing liquid of various ages is that there is no vintage system for sherry. The same barrels can be used for many years before eventually being sold to Scottish distillers who use them in whisky making, or to rum makers in the Caribbean.

The barrels attract great attention on our tour as many of those in the Fundador cellar have been signed by celebrities such as the film star Charlton Heston, and sports personalities including the golfer Seve Ballesteros, in addition to royalty from Spain and the UK. The company's website also points out that Fundador was the type of brandy drunk by the protagonists in Hemingway's 1926 novel, *The Sun Also Rises*, about a group of expatriates who travel from Paris to Spain and are transfixed when they watch a bullfight.

The basic version of sherry is fino, which is made with no intervention. Yeast – or 'flor' in the experts' vernacular – is allowed to form as a crust and causes a barrier that prevents oxygen making contact with the liquid. When this layer is removed, the residual liquid is pale yellow and dry on the palate. Each of the ensuing stages involves exposure to oxygen and the length of that exposure defines the sweetness of the flavour and intensity of the colour. The result is that amontillado is dry but slightly more complex as the build-up of alcohol kills off the flor. The other styles evolve over time to produce oloroso, manzanilla, palo cortado and Pedro Ximénez, which is darker and sweeter than the others.

We then move into the substantial Mezquita bodega next door. This is a cavernous space with room for up to 6,000 barrels. The shape of the roof and the layout of the room explain why these places are described as cathedrals.

The UK has a history of involvement in the sherry industry and that is reflected in names such as González Byass, Williams & Humbert and, in this place, Harveys. Such companies were founded as a collaboration between Spaniards and Brits, or as mergers. Fundador is now owned by a Filipino drinks company but continues to follow the traditional methods and produce sherry products that carry the Harveys label.

While many people have sherry as an aperitif, it is equally at home as an accompaniment to food, particularly tapas. Lewis and I take a table in the restaurant in order to put this to the test. We receive four sherries and a taste of the brandy, which Fundador also produces. Our drinks match a range of small dishes, starting with a rich seafood soup, and followed by a taco with tuna, mango and guacamole, pork in a barbecue sauce, pâté, and chocolate dessert. The accompanying sherries increase in intensity with each dish and our conclusion is that it is indeed a perfect foil for what we are eating.

Although it may simply be the case that the match is spot on in the case of the amontillado, it is the combination I find most enjoyable. It is amber in colour, made from Palomino grapes, and is dry. Its exposure to oxygen means it will last for longer than fino, although even amontillado would not have survived multi-year storage in granny's house. While this tasting has offered only a limited insight into the range of flavours and the versatility of sherry, my decision is made. I decide that the Harveys Amontillado will be the next addition to my wine case and buy a bottle at the bodega shop. The case is now half full.

However, while our visit and tasting have been informative and delicious, we're also here for another purpose. The Jerez race programme features a full marathon, a half-marathon and a fourteen kilometre 'promo'. We've opted for the middle of the three.

Registration the day before the race takes place at the Alcazar, the oldest existing building in Jerez. Dating back to the eleventh century, the striking silhouette is a splendid illustration of Islamic construction style. It has a mosque, an octagonal tower, attractive courtyard and well-maintained gardens plus a fine example of Arab baths. While we wait to sign on, unknowing tourists join the queue to enter the grounds, unaware that the line of people snaking around the shaded space in front of this spectacular Moorish structure is not there to appreciate the distinctive architecture. They eventually realise the error and head off in a different direction.

Once we are inside, the administration is slick and a few minutes later our names are ticked off and we're officially on the list of starters.

The event will get underway in the grounds adjacent to the Royal Andalusian School of Equestrian Art and follow the road out of town before hitting the clay paths between the vines. The average temperature for the area at this time of year is twenty-two degrees, but it's much cooler than that as we join the stream of runners strolling towards the start. The inevitable over-enthusiastic DJ pumps out loud music as a diverse field jogs and stretches and the clock ticks towards nine. Although the runners are predominantly Spanish, I discern a few other English speakers and, from the flag on their race numbers, I see that there is also a fair representation of Italians, Germans and Dutch. In all, there are 1,800 entrants spanning twenty-eight nationalities signed up to the three disciplines.

I'm aware that the course profile shows a sharp incline after around five miles and that it lasts more than a mile. On the starting line, I convince myself that if I can hold a steady pace up to that distance, I should be able to maintain my momentum on the downward stretch then aim to finish reasonably well. Perhaps that's just wishful thinking on my part.

As we set off at a gentle pace, Lewis reminds me that the last time we lined up together was in the Comic Relief Red Nose Mile while he was still at school. That wasn't yesterday. Back then, I might have expected to match him for pace, but that's a forlorn hope these days.

The first mile is the usual settling-in activity, with our speed largely regulated by the number of bodies jostling for

Switzerland. A stunning backdrop for the Marathon des Saveurs – breathtaking in more ways than one.

Switzerland: Closely packed vines show how winemakers maximise the use of available space.

Slovenia: Izola combines traditional architecture with the modernity of the boats in its harbour.

Slovenia: Waves breaking over the runners early in the race.

Slovenia: Entrance to the Parenzana Tunnel on the former railway line from Trieste to Poreč.

Slovenia: Race number showing the course profile.

Italy: A local promotion for the race.

Italy: One of the steep climbs on the route of La Prosecchina.

Italy: La Tordera vines with snow-capped peaks in the distance.

Italy: Stone building among the vines between Vidor and Valdobbiadene.

England: Enjying the winter sun at bucolic Denbies.

England: Tricky underfoot conditions for the Denbies parkrun.

Germany: Signage at the side of the course explains parkrun for locals.

Germany: The historic building where Kessler wine is made.

Spain: Race HQ and the impressive backdrop of the Alcazar.

Spain: Heading downhill towards La Trinidad winery after a gruelling climb.

Spain: A fresh-looking son with a not so fresh father just after the finish.

Spain: Barrels piled up in threes at the Fundador cellars.

Slovakia: A statue celebrating the Košice Marathon's history.

Slovakia: And they're off in Central Košice.

Portugal: Crossing the start line in the 'world's most beautiful race'.

Portugal: A welcome shower from the local fire brigade.

France: Running through the vines between Dorlisheim and Molsheim.

France: Marathon winner receiving her weight in wine.

Hungary: Setting the scene for when it gets dark.

Hungary: Headtorches at the ready for the night run.

Belgium: Dinant, home to Mr Sax.

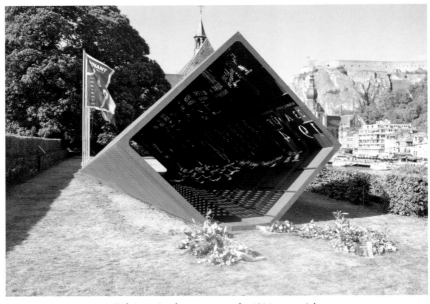

Belgium: A solemn scene at the 1914 memorial.

Belgium: Jeanette van der Steen, winemaker and human dynamo.

Belgium: Dog tired at the end of the run.

Austria: In the vines watching the Danube flow serenely by.

Austria: Perfect vantage point to watch the finishers.

Austria: As close as I'll get to a place on the podium.

The contents of Colin's Case.

a clear space and a chance to get the legs moving. An over-exuberant start by one guy means that he is already sitting on the pavement and taking a rest. We complete the first mile at roughly the pace I had hoped for, although, as the field thins out a little, I fear that our second mile may be too quick. That concern seems to be unfounded as we stride along nicely while still on the hard surface, picking off one or two of those who raced ahead in the early stages. We veer onto a gravel path and run parallel to the motorway, making steady progress until we return to the road shortly before reaching the first drinks station, around the five-mile mark. This is a chance to take on fluid, but it simply reveals another weapon that is missing from my running armoury. I'm handed a cup of water and try to combine drinking with running. I fail miserably, although thankfully the temperature is still moderate and there's no fear of dehydration at this stage.

The mood among the group changes a little and the chat ceases when we take a sharp left turn into the vines of La Trinidad vineyard. The albariza clay is ideal terrain for grapes and is famed for its drainage attributes, storing up the seasonal rain and allowing it to do its job as the growing season progresses. It's less attractive as a running surface in spring, especially after yesterday's heavy downpours. There is a name – *pergaña* – for the glutinous mud that attaches itself to our feet and makes a draining surface even more arduous.

As we ascend a daunting hill that takes the runners away from the roads and up to the highest vines in the area, the cloying mud adds several inches to my height. While that gives me a taste of life as a six-footer, I'm less impressed by the additional ballast, which makes raising my feet ever more exacting. I'm not alone, and the stiffness of the climb combines with the heavy conditions to quell any hope of running. Somewhere up ahead, one runner has slowed to a walk and the narrowness of the navigable space means that everyone else must do the same.

After almost two miles of struggling skywards, we finally crest the summit, which is marked by a religious sculpture. Then, as we head downhill towards the La Trinidad winery, we pass one runner, Antonio, who is facing the wrong way. He looks as if he is waiting for someone to complete that devilishly challenging climb. Or perhaps he has been spooked by the statue. Antonio's race number is 666.

The ground firms and we gather momentum, although the benefits of this descent fail to offset the ravages of the climb. Waiting for us at the foot of the hill, located just past the halfway point of the race, is the next feeding station. A jumble of bodies stands beside a table laden with fruit, water, bread, ham and sherry. One runner is stocking up on sandwiches – perhaps he expects to be out on the course for a while. But this race is certainly no picnic for me and, although a drop of the local speciality might be the tonic I need right now, it may just tip me over the edge, so I opt for water.

Refreshed, we head back in the direction of town. After a brief moment of feeling good, the spring has disappeared from my step and I feel the onset of cramp in my right thigh, a result of the jarring on the way down towards La Trinidad, in addition to a tightening in my troublesome Achilles. I realise that the pace at which I'm travelling is as good as it will get from here in.

We return to the gravel paths and reach a puddle that is blocking the way. Runners pass it in single file, slithering in its muddy periphery then leaping across. Long jump was my preferred field event when I was younger, but my feeble effort here would have secured very few house points in the school sports. Nevertheless, I make it to safety and we continue on our way.

Lewis has barely broken sweat, whereas I am broken and sweaty. I plod along, reassured by the beep of my watch that shows we are now only a few miles from the finish, albeit my pace is at best steady. Any possibility of being able to accelerate diminishes even further when we reach a beast of a little climb. It has caught out several of those ahead of us and they have slowed to a walk. I succumb and join them. We are almost at the peak of that hill when John jogs alongside and walks with us. He is from Cornwall and is celebrating an impressive running landmark. This is his fiftieth half-marathon.

We resume at a jog and re-enter Jerez, where a lane is coned off and the traffic is expertly managed by the police. A gentle dip takes us into the grounds of the Bodega Estevez. The doors are open and we run the length of the cellar, the oak barrels stacked high on either side of the passage blocking out the sun and creating a cool space that adds to the impression of respite and a sense of calm. The runners emerge blinking into a bright room where tables weighed down with refreshments await. Water or isotonic drinks are offered by a smiling volunteer who, perhaps sensing my need for something a little stronger, points out the availability of a reviving sherry, should I wish to partake. Once more, I decline, preferring to get back to the job at hand.

My other thigh is coming out in sympathy with its counterpart, and both are now causing me pain. Another short, sharp ascent leads to the Fundador Bodega, then the undulations continue as we pass houses where a mother and child lean out of a window to offer their encouragement.

We skirt the grounds of the González Byass Bodega, and that means we're almost within sight of the finishing line, although a policeman is not entirely honest when he encourages us by saying 'round the corner and you'll be done'. What he omits to say is that there is another climb over a cobbled surface. We pass a sizeable number of spectators whose encouragement proves to be the invisible helping hand that ensures I make it up the hill beside the Tio Pepe Bodega. I hear music and the voice of the commentator, but there's one final challenge in the shape of the dozen or so stairs we must negotiate before we reach the sanctuary of the finishing zone. Here, the blasting music is, I'm subsequently informed, 'What You Know' by Two Door Cinema Club. I have to confess that I didn't know.

The race concludes at the Alameda Vieja, a garden that is of huge cultural and historical importance. It sits amid the city's oldest grove of trees and beside the Alcazar. Lewis asks whether I can raise a sprint and I offer a poor impression of an athlete as I waddle the final fifty steps to the line. He appears as fresh as he did at the start and looks as if he could do another lap. I, by contrast, look somewhat less comfortable as I balance my hands on my aching thighs to bow my head and make it easier to receive the finisher's medal.

Water, oranges and fizzy drinks restore some semblance of normality. I note that, somewhat bizarrely, one of the post-race offerings is a bag of six carrots. Not for me, thanks, and the same is true of the latest offer of a glass of sherry. However, John has finished strongly and appears to be celebrating his considerable achievement with a drop of amontillado as he waits for his wife to complete the distance.

As I reflect on the run, I acknowledge that I knew this would be tough, particularly given the recent interruption to my training, so I'm glad to have made it round a demanding course that was actually slightly longer than the advertised half-marathon.

One man who has mastered the conditions is a local athlete, who romped home more than thirteen minutes clear of the runner-up. However, the times achieved by the leading finishers in each of the races is testament to the demanding nature of the terrain and, although I'm conscious of having struggled in the closing stages, I feel a little less disappointed with my effort when I discover that we have crossed the line almost exactly in the middle of the 600 or so who completed the half-marathon.

A quick trip back to our hotel for a shower, and we are ready to finish our morning with the breakfast we forewent a few hours ago. The sun is now gaining in strength and the people of Jerez are out in force. They're a smart-looking bunch, with dapper old men accompanying glamorously dressed women on a stroll around the lively streets or sitting outside at the many cafés and restaurants in the pedestrianised centre. As we drink our coffee, a steady flow of runners passes by, medals round their necks and a few clutching bags of carrots, with some looking more sprightly than others as they head for home.

We, too, will soon be bidding farewell to a part of Spain that for me was previously unknown. My impression of Jerez de la Frontera is of a working city with a rich history, some spectacular architecture and a strong tradition, especially in a religious context. Most of the residents we've encountered are elderly, seemingly prosperous, and generally appear to be satisfied with life.

And, of course, there's sherry. I now appreciate the distinct methods and range of styles. I certainly won't be following the tradition that existed in my youth and leaving an open bottle in my drinks cabinet.

There's one other thing I've learned from this trip. A lot of hard work lies ahead if I'm going to be ready to run the marathon I have on my schedule for five months from now.

Glass half-full moment: Discovering that sherry doesn't actually taste like my granny's offering

Glass half-empty moment: Disruption to my training made the run a real challenge

Wine selected for Colin's Case: Harveys Amontillado Jerez

Seven

SLOVAKIA

TUNE OF THE DAY:
'Pipes of Peace' — Paul McCartney

I have a Cyprus-shaped hole in my schedule. The cancellation of the trip to the island of Aphrodite means I need to find another destination with a wine-related run. Slovakia may not be a like-for-like swap, but it's an excellent substitute. Geographically, politically and in terms of its wine history, it's also similar in many ways to Moldova and therefore a reasonable replacement for another cancelled trip, although economically Slovakia is some way ahead of its neighbour. Indeed, while my destination is not yet a runaway post-independence success, the region around the Slovak capital Bratislava, is the third-wealthiest in the European Union according to some measures, and other parts of the country are following in its slipstream.

Slovakia, which in population terms is almost identical to Scotland, has a compelling history, as well as a wine industry that merits further investigation and a run that has a more interesting background than any of the others on my list.

Slavic Slovaks are believed to have first settled here in the sixth century. After being conquered by Germans and Magyars during the tenth century, Slovakia came under Hungarian control until 1918. When the First World War ended that year, Slovaks combined with other states in the region to form Czechoslovakia, which was occupied by Germany from 1939 until 1945 when it was liberated by the Soviet Union.

More than four decades of communist rule ended in 1989. A nationalist movement gathered momentum and by 1991 talks began over the Czech and Slovak republics becoming independent states. Slovakia emerged as a separate country following the Dissolution of Czechoslovakia, which became effective in January 1993. The split, which also created the Czech Republic, is often dubbed 'the Velvet Divorce' as, like the 'Velvet Revolution' that ended communist rule in Czechoslovakia, it did not involve violence or bloodshed. Slovakia joined the EU and NATO in 2004.

I'm in its second city, Košice, a place with an intriguing past that includes the engrossing story attached to the race I'm planning to run, not to mention the wine that also has a spot in the country's folklore. The city has a notable place in the history books, having been the first in Europe to have a coat of arms in 1369. That was updated by subsequent monarchs in 1423, in 1453 and again in 1502, and all of the versions are represented on the statue of an angel just inside the original city wall – rebranding, it seems, is not a new concept.

In 2022, Košice became a safe haven for many refugees from neighbouring Ukraine fleeing Russian bombs and bullets. In that context, the title Peace Half-Marathon is apt for the event

I have entered. The run is a spin-off from a globally recognised race. The Peace Marathon dates to 1924 when Béla Braun, a journalist from Košice who later changed his name to Vojtech Braun Bukovský, attended the Olympic Games in Paris. He was inspired by the dramatic nature of the marathon, a race won by Finland's Albin Stenroos in searing Parisian heat that meant almost half the field failed to finish. On his return home, Braun set about organising a similar event, and the inaugural Peace Marathon took place later that year with eight participants. It is now Europe's longest-established marathon.

The race has grown in size and stature, attracting some of the world's leading exponents of distance running. Charged with the organisational task is Marathon Club Košice, which was formed in 1990 and has assumed responsibility for ensuring the survival of an event that continues to thrive, as well as supporting the growth of athletics across Slovakia.

The race still takes place each October, but there is now a second associated date on the racing calendar. In May, a half-marathon and a quarter-marathon take place. Given that it took my legs almost a week to recover from my Spanish adventure, and the fact that I have another half-marathon on the agenda within a few weeks, I have opted for the shorter distance. It still promises to be a decent test of whether I've regained full fitness following the recent blip.

My first impressions are formed on the 23 bus. By coincidence, it's the same number as the service I use most frequently at home. However, that's where the similarities end. While the Edinburgh version runs between two of the Scottish capital's residential areas, the Košice service starts at the airport, where the continental habit of refusing to queue is evidently part of the landscape. A gaggle of travellers recently disembarked from incoming flights sprawls around the terminus waiting for the vehicle to arrive. I clutch the ticket I have just bought from a machine with the help of a local, and naively expect to have to register it on the machine inside the bus, as the rules require. The driver pulls in and opens all three doors, sparking a scrap featuring arms and elbows, and involving strategic use of bags, as passengers ignore the ticket protocol, declining to use the stamp machine in favour of battling it out for the seats. I choose the path of least resistance, boarding at the back and opting to stand.

As the bus wends its way towards the city, the most striking aspect of the scenery is a construction style dating back to the communist era, and a forest of high-rise flats that tell of a working city where buildings are designed to maximise accommodation in a limited space. It is a relatively short journey and we are soon at the terminus where stepping off the bus is a little more orderly.

Reaching my hotel entails a walk through the Mestský Park (translated as City Park), a substantial green space that is home to many facilities and activities, with users of all ages walking, playing sports or using it as a short cut to the Old Town.

The contrasts I see on my first exploratory stroll tell of a city still in transition, with a vibrant young population driving modernisation in an aspirational society where everything is not yet evolving at a consistent pace and there are, to my eye at least, some social problems. Nevertheless, the good outweighs the bad and Košice's historical centre features a conservation area defined by its majestic architecture, with buildings that reflect the mediaeval period when these impressive structures were home to royalty. Around the heart of the city, memorials tell of a history that has seen Košice come under the influence of many nationalities, and help to explain how it has changed its name as often as a serial bride. It has been labelled in German, Hungarian, Turkish, French, Romanian, Polish and Russian, among others. Running adjacent to the main pedestrianised zone are numerous lanes, which house museums and workshops occupied by artisans, while the cultural heart is marked out by the original city walls.

Košice is an ancient city, with documents from the early thirteenth century showing that it was originally called Villa Kassa. It has gone through various iterations before becoming the place that it is today. On the face of it, it is economically vibrant, boasting a youthful population of around 240,000, with an average age of just over thirty-five. The centre is traffic-free and most of the commerce is either traditional or tourist-focused. However, modern retail is encroaching, and there are recently opened shopping centres at either end of Hlavná ulica, the pedestrianised main street running through the Old Town. It is a busy thoroughfare that swaps its clientele in the evening when the groups of schoolchildren and the tour parties have gone, strolling becomes the activity of choice, and the bars and restaurants fill with thirsty drinkers and hungry diners. People-watching is a favoured pastime and the entertainment includes observing cyclists seeking to avoid pedestrians, and vice versa.

A couple of streets back, I sit at an outdoor restaurant table and observe spruced-up couples heading for their dinner reservations, while a moneyed boy racer whizzes by in a BMW convertible. I also see families that are clearly struggling, rummaging through rubbish that has been deposited outside a shop. Thankfully such incidents are rare and, at the time of my visit, the national unemployment rate is less than seven per cent.

The city's main employer is an American-owned steelworks, US Steel Košice, and industrial jobs account for much of the local workforce. The company is among the major sponsors of the Peace Half-Marathon, and I will later note from signs outside the neo-baroque State Theatre that it is also a supporter of the city's vibrant arts scene, which presents a range of shows, events and exhibitions.

In addition to learning about Košice's rich and evolving culture, my trip presents an opportunity to experience another aspect of the country's colourful past that has spilled into its present and plays an increasingly influential role in creating the foundations on which to form a prosperous future. On this occasion, there is no direct link between the race and the region's wine, but the same historical connection that applies to the evolution of the city exists in the country's wine industry. Košice is renowned for vinification, but I'm sure Slovakia has much more to offer than what is available locally. Delving into the traditions confirms this to be the case. And this looks to be an ideal place to sample wines from the various regions of a nation that borrows a great deal from its better-known neighbours, yet has its own idiosyncrasies. I'm intrigued.

Most Slovak wine comes from the south of the country and is made from grapes grown on the banks of the Danube. Production is spread across six of the country's eight regions. I'm in one of those, the East Slovak Wine Region – or Východoslovenská vinohradnícka oblast, as the Slovakians say – but I've found a way to try wines from some of the other five as well. My lack of linguistic insight into this part of the world means I'll have to stick with the English versions of that handful, so Little Carpathians, South Slovak, Nitra, Central Slovak and Tokaj wine regions will suffice for my purposes. The latter, which takes in Košice, has had a long-lasting dispute with neighbouring Hungary over the rights to the Tokaj name. That feud now appears to have been resolved, with the EU ruling that both countries have a right to use the title to describe their sweet wine. Nevertheless, it's a small player in the Slovak wine industry as a whole, and I'm more excited to learn about the nation's other offerings.

Many of the grape varieties date back to Austro-Hungarian times. Records emphasise the importance of Košice's role in the wine industry. Documents from 1521 show that wine formed part of the remuneration of professionals such as merchants, doctors, lawyers and clerics. It also made an important contribution to Košice's revenues. Much of that income was generated by a bar, known as Levoča House. It remains in existence today and continues to generate income, much of it in the form of tourist euros, although it now has the name Hostinec and features a microbrewery.

Among the more acclaimed Slovak producers is Peter Matyšák. His winery is at Pezinok, around 250 miles from Košice. He uses grapes from vineyards in two of the winemaking regions, Little Carpathians and South Slovakia. That spread ensures Matyšák wines are a fair representation of several varieties and styles.

He is a dynamic businessman and, in addition to seeking international outlets for his wine, he has sought ways to broaden exposure in the domestic market. One of the techniques he employs is to welcome visitors to the company's headquarters near the Slovak capital, Bratislava, which is in the west of the country, some seven hours away by train. However, the enterprising Mr Matyšák has also built a network of wine shops, one of which is just over half a mile from my hotel. That's an ideal way to seek advice on wines from the Košice region and beyond, and to identify the next bottle for my case. I have a visit pencilled in for after my race.

Several of the runs I have completed so far are embedded in my memory as a result of the local characteristics – vines occupying every available space, low-energy street lighting that creates an atmospheric mood, or the high number of religious buildings. Košice has staked its claim. From now, I will recall it as the city of fountains. No park or garden, it seems, is complete without at least one installation. Even my hotel has a water cascade as a contribution to its eco status – it also has various energy-saving and environmental measures in place to bolster its green credentials.

Of the many water-based attractions, the one that draws the largest audience is the Singing Fountain, which gushes in time to music. The benches in the adjacent gardens are constantly occupied by walkers taking a moment to relax, families with children, and tourists or office workers enjoying a picnic lunch. A city employee also uses it to ostentatiously underline his importance as guardian of the fountain. He switches off the waterflow then theatrically removes, cleans and replaces the lightbulbs, poking a metal prod into the gubbins to ensure the sprinkle is maximised when he chooses to restore the service. He has done a fine job on the basis of the display that takes place when he hits the restart button to produce a string of favourites that wows the audience – 'The Winner Takes It All' by Abba brings on a mighty spurt, while I fear that 'I'm Still Standing' by Elton John will never be the same again without the associated water show.

The Singing Fountain sits in front of the State Theatre building, and is just a few paces from St Elizabeth's Cathedral, Slovakia's oldest place of worship. I decide to climb the bell tower, which is dedicated to St Urban, the patron saint of people who work in the wine industry. I'm rewarded for the effort of climbing the steep, narrow staircase by a panoramic view over the city.

I decide to investigate what the buildings on the horizon are. The tourist office is an obvious source of more information. English is spoken here, but I'm surprised at the unbridled enthusiasm of the two staff – one a girl in her early thirties, the other a little younger – as they respond to my 'hello'. They seem thrilled to have an opportunity to put their language skills to use and are great ambassadors for Košice.

They give me a map of the city plus another that covers the whole region, and one of the duo leads me to a shelved unit stuffed with leaflets in Slovak, German and English, then tells me to take anything I want. I pick up a couple of brochures and go back to the desk. At this point, it feels as if I have stumbled onto the set of *Columbo*, the television detective, whose crime-solving skills are defined by his insistence on asking just one more question.

My conversation with the younger of the two assistants starts with her asking:

'Did you find something useful?'

'Yes, thank you.'

'One more thing – where are you from? It's for our records.'

'I'm from Scotland.'

'One more thing – do you want some coffee or water?'

'Could I have some water please?'

'Here is your water. One more thing – would you like me to recommend places to visit?'

At this point I opt out and decide to make my own enquiries. I've picked up enough information to keep me occupied for a couple of days. One more thing I learned from them, though – apparently, the correct pronunciation of Košice is Co-she-say.

Among the structures detailed in my newly acquired literature stash is the Peace Marathon Statue, which was created by a local sculptor, Arpád Račko, to mark the thirtieth anniversary of the event. It features on the route of the run, as I discover when I go to collect my race number, which is delivered in an envelope with the course printed on it. I notice that the guy who offered me ticket-buying advice at the airport is also at the sign-on. I wanted to call him Kenny given his facial resemblance to someone I know of that name. However, I will later discover that this is Jakub.

I am up early on race day after a troubled sleep. The usual concerns about missing the alarm are multiplied by nagging doubts over whether my Achilles will allow me to take part, although a jog around Mestský Park as a pre-race fitness test has offered me some reassurance. I stretch for an hour before leaving the hotel and tread warily as I make my way to the start.

Some serious-looking dudes are warming up in the side streets and crowds are assembling around the start near the cathedral in the Old Town, with musical accompaniment provided by a drumming band. Runners over the two distances combine and different-coloured numbers distinguish the half-marathoners from those who have opted for the shorter race – the longer run is two laps of the same course. The 700 or so starters are sent on their way, with the narrow space meaning that it takes me almost a minute to cross the line, although chip timing means that the additional seconds will be deducted at the end to produce an accurate clocking for the run.

We jostle to avoid the tram lines and evade others – I've noticed that Slovaks are not great at spatial awareness, a generalisation perhaps, but an observation based on what appears to be a recurring habit of failing to make way for other pedestrians, even in tight spaces. I'm again conscious of that as the heaving mass bobbles towards the open space at the edge of the Old Town and one runner at my elbow forces another to step in front of me and we make contact, although the impact is not enough to cause a problem.

The first mile is slower than the schedule I had set as my target when submitting my entry, but the main observation is that my Achilles is easing. My pace remains steady as we pass the Peace Marathon Statue onto a wide road that allows everyone enough space to find a rhythm. We sweep left into a built-up area that is characterised by high-rise buildings.

As we approach the three kilometre sign, a girl sprints past and veers towards the side of the road then begins waving frantically and shouting. A woman, probably the runner's grandmother, is on a fourth-floor balcony and shouts a word or two of encouragement before the girl re-joins the group.

A DJ has set up at a junction that runners will pass three times and is blasting out what to my uneducated ears sounds like something that should perhaps have been Slovakia's Eurovision entry. We head off on a small loop that means we meet the leaders travelling in the opposite direction. We complete the mini circuit and retrace our steps. We pass the music man once more several minutes later and my assessment is that he may or may not be playing a different tune.

The temperature is bearable but is rising and the halfway point brings the welcome sight of a water station. It also gives me another opportunity to practise my skills of consumption on the run. I slow to little more than a walk in order to limit the spillage. It's difficult to say whether that was any improvement on my efforts in Spain, but the liquid is gratefully received, and strikes more of a chord than the music, which still sounds the same as we pass for the third time.

The run is almost completely flat and, for those at the front at least, relatively fast. The next two miles involve an out-and-back section along a wide boulevard where dog walkers and strollers stop to offer encouragement.

I'm moving steadily, while purposefully trying to avoid provoking my Achilles, which is uncomfortable but not painful. For that reason, I have abandoned any hope of achieving my target and instead I'm moving at the pace I would hope to achieve over the full marathon distance. It is satisfying to note that each of my miles is slightly quicker than the preceding one.

We approach the Peace Marathon Statue from a different angle and pass it again. It names previous winners and the roll of honour features marathon royalty such as Abebe Bekele – the barefoot Ethiopian star of the 1960s – Derek Clayton – the Australian who took the world record to new levels at the end of that decade – and more recently, as a sign of African dominance in the event this millennium, a string of winners from Kenya and Ethiopia.

The richness of that list, combined with the slickness of today's organisation, underlines why Košice enjoys such esteemed status on the global running map, although some parts of the route are far from picturesque. The surroundings become easier on the eye once we are back inside the city walls and the familiar surroundings of Hlavná ulica. Café customers take time out from their early morning refreshments and encourage flagging runners to raise the pace along the home straight. The ten kilometre sign means I'm almost there, and the sound of a drumbeat accompanies me towards the finish – straight ahead for quarter-marathoners and a left turn for those whose second lap looms.

I am relatively comfortable as I cross the line, and a bottle of water soon has me functioning fully and ready to return to the hotel to shower and change. By the time I get there, I've had a text with my finishing time. I have run steadily and a subsequent glance at the breakdown shows that I managed to accelerate in the closing stages. And, somewhat surprisingly, I discover that I finished comfortably in the top half of the field and was second in my age category.

It is now coffee time and I head back into town then find a table with a prime view to watch the tailenders in the half-marathon. I notice that Jakub, who has a finishers' medal round his neck, has made his way to the roadside to encourage a woman whom I assume is his mother, as she struggles along the cobbled final mile.

With the road closures restricted to three hours in order to limit the disruption, marshals on foot and on bicycles help to pace the slower finishers towards the line. The last lady still out on the course earns cheers and applause as she concludes her run. And with two minutes to spare before the cut-off, an elderly man puffs past. It is unlikely he'll make the deadline, but I check later and he has been credited with a finishing time that is fifty-one seconds outside the limit.

Before I've walked back along the street, the cones that blocked the road have been gathered, the fencing removed and work has started on dismantling the gantry. Some volunteers are already ensconced in adjacent bars sipping a well-deserved beer. By the afternoon, all the race paraphernalia has gone and the start/finish area near the underground museum, Dolna Brana (Lower Gate), at the eastern edge of the Old Town, is back to normal.

Part of my race-day routine is to buy a local newspaper. On this occasion my quest produces limited results. I have bought one that is a weekend publication containing a series of long-read type articles and I also pick up *Nový Čas*, the only one I can find bearing today's date. It is the country's best-selling tabloid and has a picture of Madonna on the back page, although I'm not sure what she has been up to, even with the help of an online translation tool. Košice is the first place I have visited where I have not seen a single person reading a newspaper, or even carrying one – maybe that is a consequence of the city having a young population. On further investigation it seems that those journals that do exist are all printed in Bratislava. I have seen only one newsstand, while newsagents in Košice are rare and appear to be used almost exclusively as lottery ticket sales outlets.

I am heading back towards the main part of town when I spot a familiar couple coming towards me. It is them – Jakub and the woman I assume is his mother. This is a city with almost a quarter of a million people and that number is inflated this weekend by runners and supporters, as well as other visitors. And, although the centre comprises only a couple of streets, it seems bizarre that I should keep meeting the first Slovak I spoke to.

Around me, the bars are doing a lively trade. While beer is the drink of choice for lots of Slovaks and comes in an array of colours, flavours and strengths, wine has long been a staple of the local economy and the preference for many people. Most of Slovakia's wine goes no further than the domestic market and, of the rest, the Czech Republic is the main export destination.

My research before coming to Košice showed that grape varieties have a heavy Austrian influence. That is good news as far as I am concerned, as I believe that wines from there are often underrated. The most planted white grape in Slovakia is Veltlínské zelené, a close relative of Grüner Veltliner, and the top red, Frankovka modrá, is better known in the wine world as Blaufränkisch. I also learn of a red variety known as Dunaj, which takes its name from the Slovak word for the Danube. It is a combination of three grapes, Muscat Bouchet, Oporto and St Laurent, and is a sign that, while foreign influences are strong, aspects of the Slovak wine industry are unique.

As with other countries I've visited over recent months, Slovakia serves wine in 100 millilitre measures, although my experience here suggests that it is common practice for bars and restaurants to offer a double measure. My investigation begins at a place in the Old Town that is known for its great wines. I order a glass of Dunaj together with two local cheeses, which prove to be a good match for what is in my glass.

My next sampling comes in the evening when I opt for Frankovka modrá to accompany my dinner. This is rich and fruity. To help narrow the alternatives, I also try a white from the winemaker Nichta, which is based at Čajkov in the Nitra region. It is a nice wine, but I think the reds I have tried are a little more specific to Slovakia so that is what I'll be adding to my case, although I will seek some guidance before making a final decision. Taking a lengthy train trip to the vineyards in Pezinok would entail a commitment that is unfeasible given the length of my stay, so I track down Matyšák's shop to a modern shopping centre just beyond the Old Town's eastern perimeter.

Matyšák boasts a modern winery, which was built in 2002 to replace the existing building and houses cutting-edge facilities that are ideal for creating high-quality wine. The previous winery became a restaurant that is renowned in the Pezinok area. A cellar was subsequently added to the new facility and this is where the wine matures in oak barrels. Matyšák works with growers in the Lesser Carpathian and South Slovak regions, buying their grapes, which are then used to create the wine that is sold in a range of outlets, including the shop in Košice.

I'm served by Eva, whose English is only a little better than my non-existent Slovak. Shelves groan with bottles from across the Matyšák range, so I seek her help. She recommends the Prestige Gold Frankovka modrá 2017 and I'm happy to go with her choice. It's similar in age to the glass I enjoyed with dinner and comes in a bottle with a golden silhouette of Peter Matyšák and a huge slab of text on the label. All bottles in Slovakia show the region, in this case Malokarpatská, the district, which is Hlohovec, and the vineyard, Šomod. An online translator tells me that the grapes come from a sixty-year-old vineyard, and the wine is dark pink with an aroma of cherries, tobacco and chocolate, and a full flavour with the aftertaste of coffee. Sounds good.

With the bottle carefully packed, I'm ready to bring my Slovak sojourn to a close, and I head for the station. This time there is no need for Kenny/Jakub to help me negotiate the ticket machine. I am now familiar with the 23 bus, which is busy on the half-hour journey to the airport, not with suitcase-toting tourists, but with workers heading for the first shift of the week at the technology and engineering factories on the edge of the city.

My assessment of Košice is that it is a place with a fascinating history, a stunning Old Town and, of course, a race that enjoys a worthy place in the almanac of great running events. It has a vibrant young population and a thriving tourist industry. Basing my view purely on the experience of my brief visit, I think the best way to sum up the city is to apply a wine analogy. It is still a little young and immature but should evolve over the next five to ten years to become an attractive contender for the consumer's money. That is also true of its wine.

Glass half-full moment: Discovering a fascinating place with a compelling history

Glass half-empty moment: Struggling to shake off the troublesome Achilles problem

Wine selected for Colin's Case: Matyšák Prestige Gold Frankovka modrá 2017

Eight

PORTUGAL

TUNE OF THE DAY:
'Into the Valley' – The Skids

*T*he scenery is breath-taking as I travel towards the next stop on my schedule. I'm heading for Portugal's Douro Valley, a couple of hours by train from Porto, the country's second-largest city after Lisbon.

Port, of course, is a big deal in this part of the world, but it's not the only consideration when it comes to identifying the next bottle for my case. Indeed, table wine production here has closed the gap on its fortified alternative, and I'm heading into the valley hoping to gain an insight as to why that change is taking place.

Wine has been made here for more than 2,000 years and the region has Portugal's highest wine classification – Denominação de Origem Controlada (DOC). Port has been crucial to the fortunes of the area for much of that period. As ever, where there is money to be made, it has also been targeted by a few scoundrels and scandals, particularly in the early part of the eighteenth century. That questionable activity led to action in 1756 by the Marquês de Pombal, the Portuguese prime minister of that era.

His stock was high after he helped Lisbon recover from a devastating earthquake that had destroyed much of the city. He then turned his attention to the port trade and formed a company that assumed control of the industry, effectively transferring it into state ownership. Pombal implemented a grading system for port that resulted in classifications that allowed better wines to be sold for higher prices and exported, while poorer produce was destined only for the domestic market. His action was a precursor to the categorisations that would follow in Bordeaux around a century later. The Pombal rules have changed a bit over the years, but still form the spine of current regulations in Portugal.

His intervention helped the area become the heartland for Portuguese wine exports and fuelled the growth of Peso da Régua, a place that now has around 17,000 inhabitants spread across the town and surrounding districts on the western edge of the Alto Douro. Wine was traditionally made here and transported downstream to Porto in barrels loaded onto flat-bottomed boats known as *rabelos*. Régua's industrial history is told at the Museu do Douro, a wine-focused museum that is located beside the river in a street named after the Marquês de Pombal.

The rise in popularity of port during the eighteenth century left still wines as the poor relation and the idea that it was of inferior quality became a self-fulfilling prophesy. The time it took for boats to negotiate the distance to Porto, and the absence of navigable roads or railways also contributed to the lack of demand. The arrival in Régua of the first train in 1879 was a catalyst for change, facilitating movement of people and goods, most notably fortified wine.

That situation persisted for several centuries and only started to change in the 1990s when the DOC categorisation was broadened to include both still wines and port. The change provided the spur to increase production levels.

These days, fruity reds and bone-dry whites represent a growing proportion of the output in the Douro and are increasingly acknowledged by wine experts. The recent upturn in quality has helped to shed the reputation of unfortified wine production as a side activity in a region where making port is the real business. Another reputational boost arrived with the growth in wine tourism, which has opened up the Alto Douro region and made it into a regular stopping point on river cruises.

Caroline, who some in the know might describe as my long-suffering wife, has joined me for this trip. She is here as non-playing captain in terms of the run, but I expect her to provide useful input on the wine selection. Her presence also means the accommodation budget is bumped up a little from when I journey solo. We are travelling from Porto on a two-hour train trip that reveals the spectacular landscape and explains why UNESCO awarded the area World Heritage status in 2001.

Boarding the train at Campanhã station involves climbing a step that gives a whole new meaning to the warning, 'mind the gap', and an elderly lady asks for help with the manoeuvre before taking her seat in the spacious carriage.

Those passengers in the know sit on the right-hand side as the train trundles past high-rise flats, then skirts more substantial homes in Porto's leafier suburbs and eventually crosses the city boundary. These people will benefit from the glorious views that lie ahead. We have erred by opting for seats on the left.

The distances between buildings increase a little and nature takes over as we pass a series of small towns, each slightly more agricultural than the last. A horse nonchalantly swishes away the flies with a casual tail swing in one of the rare signs of life, and the number of people declines, with the station personnel among the few that we see over the rest of the journey.

As we tick off the stops, the sky opens out and the verdant scene leaves passengers with their noses against the windows, gazing upwards towards the riverside peaks and taking in the postcard-worthy views. The track dips to river level just after the town of Mosteirô and, at Arêgos, oranges and lemons grow beside the track, while boats are tied up near waterside houses, offering a peaceful scene that is shared by the people on the cruise ships that chug gently on their way to the same towns and vineyards that are the ultimate destination for some of the passengers on the train.

Perfect rows of vines grow on sheer slopes that fill the landscape from the cloudless sky to the glistening river in a configuration that aims to maximise the available space for growing grapes. The lines of blossoming plants are uniformly spectacular and use either stone walls to produce narrow, walled terraces, known as *socalcos*, or the system known as *patamares*, which are cut into the hillsides to mark the boundaries of individual plots, and were described by the renowned historian and geographer, Orlando Ribeiro, as the most impressive man-made Portuguese construction.

The soil is stony and composed primarily of schist, which heats up when the sun is at its peak and is a key element in producing intense wines. The vines were reshaped after the attack by the phylloxera bug that almost wiped out the wine industry across Europe in the second half of the nineteenth century. As with other countries seeking a remedy, Portugal used a system of grafting local vines onto American roots that were resistant to the disease. Regional grape varieties now flourish and grow in compact bunches, producing small, sweet fruit that results in the concentrated flavours that are evident in Portuguese wines.

We are now in the Alta Douro region. Clinging to the hills are numerous little houses, which seem to be defying gravity, and *quintas*, the estates that are responsible for producing wine. As impressive as the engineering that has gone into building them is the effort that must go into harvesting the grapes. Some quintas follow the full routine of growing, harvesting and maturing the grapes, while others produce such limited amounts that it is more economically viable to send the ripe fruit to independent makers who will complete the activity on behalf of the owners, or to co-operatives where they will be combined with those from other small growers.

My first thought as I weigh up the magnificence of the scenery is that the valley may funnel heat that could make it uncomfortable terrain for the half-marathon I have entered. The weather forecast also supports that view, with prospects of a sweaty morning prompting race organisers to announce an increase in the frequency of water stations, which will now be placed at one-and-a-half-mile intervals.

We arrive in the quaintly outmoded station at Régua, which is a working town that appears to be undergoing a renaissance judging by the amount of construction and renovation work taking place. It looks richly endowed with bridges across the Douro. The streets are largely untouched by international retail chains, and the traditional outlets that exist have a typical Iberian bias towards hairdressers and shoe shops – Spaniards and Portuguese are invariably well-coiffed and well-shod. There is also an indoor market, the usual clutch of pharmacists and a couple of mini supermarkets, alongside an ironmongers with an impressive range of ironing boards that have been splayed across a large section of the pavement. As we stroll on the shaded side of the street, I note that the whole town has bought into the importance of the weekend's event. Offices and shops display the red official race T-shirt, some employing striking creativity to incorporate it into an otherwise mundane window layout.

While much of Régua goes about its day-to-day life in unspectacular fashion, there are some prominent buildings that hint at a meaningful past – and potentially a prosperous future as wine tourism attracts visitors and their euro-stuffed wallets. Religious buildings retain their former glories and the centre of town is home to the imposing four-storey public library. It opened in its current form in 2006, having previously been the Palacete dos Barretos, which was built in the nineteenth century. Meanwhile, blue signs with yellow arrows are a reminder that Régua is on the Caminho Português, the name of the pilgrimage paths that begin in Portugal and lead to the Spanish town of Santiago de Compostela.

The Museu do Douro's exhibits tell of port's importance in the region's history. They also explain the growth of non-fortified table wines. Portugal has more than 250 grape varieties, and in the Douro the number is around eighty. That said, it looks as if most vineyards have far fewer than that. Dry reds account for the bulk of still wine, with Touriga Nacional, Touriga Franca, Tinta Barroca, Tinto Cao and Tinta Roriz the most widely planted vines. Whites, which are light and refreshing, tend to rely on Malvasia Fina, Rabigato, Viosinho and Gouveio grapes. Wall-mounted text in the museum encapsulates the evolution of the local table wines alongside the sweet, dessert version for which the region is best known, saying, 'Today, Port and Douro wines are a perfect match of ancestral knowledge and modern technology'.

The museum is also race headquarters. There's a bustle of anticipation as runners sign on and collect a bag that contains their race number, T-shirt, sponsors' blurb and, just in case we forget what the area is famous for, a bottle of port. The event carries the title EDP Meia Maratona do Douro Vinhateiro. That last word, which translates as 'winegrower', is the reason it is on my list. All the race publicity and the posters draped over public spaces around the town carry a strapline that describes it as 'A Mais Bela Corrida Do Mundo'. Whether there is any substance to the assertion that it is the world's most beautiful race is unclear, but there is no doubt that the route along the riverside looks stunning.

Race day will allow me to make my own assessment on the accuracy of the claim. First, I have to get to the starting line at Barragem de Bagaúste, a dam three miles outside town. Organisers have a slick set-up that allows runners to book travel when submitting a race entry. A reminder of the train reservation is printed on my race number, so there is no excuse for being late. There is also a fleet of buses operating a shuttle service for those with no train reservation.

A glance at previous results shows that this is a fast race. I have checked the profile, so I know that, although the course follows the river – and includes a bridge that crosses it a mile or so from the finish – there are a couple of testing little climbs that come in the closing miles. On the advice of a physio, I haven't trained properly for two weeks in the hope of calming my Achilles problem. I've jogged a little, walked a bit and ridden a static bike in order to keep ticking over. In current sporting parlance, I'm a bit undercooked.

In reality, that is the least accurate way to describe how I'm feeling as I walk/jog the couple of miles to Régua station under a sun that is already radiating a lot of heat. I cross the pedestrian bridge – once part of the railway but now a wood-slatted, traffic-free area with spectacular views to the river – and look down on a small settlement of camper vans that has sprouted overnight. Presumably it is home to runners who will be joining me for the race. I arrive at the station a little ahead of schedule and catch an earlier train, meaning I have around two and a half hours to kill until we get underway. I can feel the sun on my back as I stretch my muscles while watching a cruise ship pass serenely by with passengers enjoying an early-morning coffee on deck. It occurs to me that I forgot to slather sunblock on my unaccustomed Scottish skin before I left the accommodation. I hope that won't prove too serious an oversight.

Meanwhile, the later trains and buses deposit the predominantly red-clad stream of more than 3,000 competitors who gather on the bridge where the start will take place for both the half-marathon and the five kilometre fun run. We will go left and head further away from Régua before turning for home. The runners who have signed up for the shorter event will go right. Some have taken the notion of fun a little further than others, with one group enjoying a picnic including glasses of sparkling wine before taking their place in the line-up, while a woman concludes her warm-up by stubbing out her cigarette then joining the group. I set off for a jog to keep my legs ticking over and meet a group of yellow-clad supporters who have fired up a barbecue, with the head chef swigging from a bottle of beer as he waits for the charcoal to heat. It is not yet nine o'clock.

There are almost forty nationalities and a broad range of abilities in the half-marathon field, with an elite group given preferential spots on the start line to ensure they are not held back in the serious contest that will unfold at the sharp end in the battle for the 850 euro top prize. The rest of us jostle for a space, some working their way to the front and attracting knowing glances from others who recognise the over-optimism of racing novices.

I'm somewhere in the middle of the field as we ease into action. The opening mile passes without incident and a large group remains concertinaed as we approach the first refreshment station. The scouts who had welcomed us from the train have now been redeployed as water boys and girls, ensuring plenty of fluid is available as the temperature continues to climb. Of course, hydration comes with consequences, and runners disappear into the bushes at regular intervals.

Overall, it is a good-humoured bunch and that extends to some of the spectators, with one lady appearing at the end of her drive to offer encouragement. And ensuring that her sage words are heard by all, she uses a megaphone to generate volume that catches one runner ahead by surprise, causing a startled reaction and much hilarity.

My creaking muscles are holding up reasonably well, although I sense that tougher times lie ahead. I am running alongside Manuel. He goes past on several occasions and seems to be leaving me behind. However, he then slows and I manage to reel him in then regain the initiative. While we languish somewhere in the middle of the field, at the front the leaders have already reached the mid-point and the two leaders are going at a fair lick as they pass on the other side of the road on target to complete the distance in around sixty-five minutes.

Several minutes later, my mini group approaches the furthest point on the thirteen-mile course and we prepare to turn back and retrace our steps towards the start. Ahead, I see the distinctive livery of a fire engine. It turns out that the town's *bombeiros* have been summoned to help minimise the risk to the runners of temperatures that are now heading past thirty and will eventually peak another five or six degrees above that level. The truck is strategically placed to allow its hose to deliver cooling jets of water. They are well-received and a couple of people come to a standstill to maximise the benefits before splashing back into action.

The route, which is now following the edge of the river, is still relatively flat and the scenery is striking. From behind, I hear a female voice urging everyone to take in the vertiginous slopes that reach skywards on the far side of the Douro, which flows serenely past a few metres from the edge of the road – 'mir', she shouts to her Portuguese compatriots. And for the benefit of all others, she translates her exhortations into English, 'lift your eyes'.

She is, of course, correct. It is easy to focus on the road rising ahead rather than the surroundings. The heat is the issue and I chuckle at the chorus of relief from my group when we round a bend to find the shadow cast by a small clump of trees and the even more welcome sensation of a breeze that offers temporary respite before the sun resumes its relentless glare as we climb a gentle incline towards the ninth mile.

In the distance I hear sirens. They grow louder and eventually three ambulancemen on motorbikes race towards us. They come to a halt a little way ahead of me, where a disturbing scene is unfolding as a runner lies motionless and receives CPR. We move to the other side of the road as directed and carry on. I am no longer bemoaning my discomfort. A second ambulance is parked a little further ahead and is dealing with another incident, although this one appears less serious.

We are now passing the dam where the race started and I know I have three miles left. I am completely spent, and this home stretch will take me a while. I am still overtaking some runners but I have the feeling that for each one I pass, two get the better of me and I am rapidly losing places overall. A second shower from the fire brigade brings another splattering of relief and I seize every bottle of water I am offered at the feeding stations, drinking some and dousing myself with the rest.

My personal rivals at this point still include Manuel, whose pace appears to be slowing even more than mine, and Ana, who overtook me earlier but stopped at a water station, allowing me to catch up. We pass each other several times before Ana disappears into the distance, while Manuel draws away before slowing to a walk that allows me to catch him and eventually shake him off.

Meanwhile, two mates are demonstrating that teamwork doesn't always pay off. One of them is in good shape, the other struggling to continue. It's like a series of comedy sketches as the healthier one cajoles his friend. A spurt takes them past ten or so runners but fatigue causes another halt and they lose all their gains. The same action is repeated a few times before, in a final desperate effort, they overtake us once more. The fresher runner now has his hand squarely in the centre of his pal's back and is pushing. That generates a brief spell of momentum, but it soon peters out. Frustration takes over and one heads up the road, while the other slows to a crawl and is left to his own devices.

I am on familiar territory as we enter Régua. I cross the wooden-slatted footbridge where the breeze is back in the form of a crosswind that buffets the runners as we turn left onto the final downhill mile. The roads are lined with spectators standing alongside those who have already finished and are returning to the village of campervans.

The finish is visible in the distance. I manage to raise the pace to little more than a plod and less than half a mile from the line I encounter another bombeiro. He is having fun as he directs his jets of water directly at the runners. I am struck by a cooling spritz, which, combined with the headwind and my ragged state, almost halts me in my tracks. I trundle on and stumble over the line. It has been a tough morning, and my time is poor, meaning I finish outside the top half of the runners in my age category. However, I have made it and another of my twelve runs is done.

A first-aid worker eyes me cautiously, perhaps thinking that the old guy is looking unhealthily shaky on his feet. She would be correct, although more water helps me to regain a degree of normality. There's a huge queue for the on-site physio, so I pass on the chance to have my Achilles stretched and rubbed, and head for the exit, stopping to collect a beer from a sponsor's van.

Caroline is at our pre-arranged meeting point nearby. This isn't the first time in our relationship that I have arrived at a rendezvous later than planned. She has been standing in the baking sun but I think she understands that I got here as quickly as I could. I present her with the beer as scant compensation for her patience, and we head back to our accommodation – a task that is easier for her than it is for me as fatigue takes its toll.

The race, of course, is only part of the reason for coming to a part of the world I would probably never have otherwise visited. My attention turns to choosing bottle number eight for my case. This is not the formality I had anticipated. Despite Régua's historical links to the port industry, the fortified wine is not a shoo-in. There are numerous contenders among the excellent local table wines, and a couple of other factors help me towards a conclusion.

The first is a note in the museum stating that table wines were traditionally produced for private consumption, often using inferior grapes, but are now gaining traction on the global market as their quality improves. Port has always been produced for export, and the UK was traditionally the biggest buyer, although that is no longer the case. France now accounts for around one-quarter of sales, while Brits consume around half of that amount.

Régua is home to the head office of the trade body, IVDP – Instituto dos Vinhos do Douro e do Porto – which also has an office in Porto. The institute has its own lab and a tasting panel, the Camara dos Provadores, which ensures standards are maintained, and publishes data relating to the production and sales of both styles. Recent numbers show that port sales still exceed those of table wines, but there is now very little between the two.

An article in the weekend edition of the *Nascer Do Sol* newspaper tells how the trend of celebrities putting their names to table wines has reached this part of Portugal. Among the global names highlighted in the piece are Jon Bon Jovi, George Clooney and Sarah Jessica Parker, a trio whose contribution to the wine industry in various parts of the world is firmly established. A little less well covered by the international media, as the article points out, is the involvement of Portuguese football star Nuno Ribeiro – better known to supporters of the clubs he represented, including Chelsea, as Maniche. He has a partnership with a local vineyard, Quinta da Pacheca, to produce Dezoito by Maniche, in recognition of the number eighteen shirt he wore during his career.

Instead of booking in to test Maniche's offering, we visit a wine shop in the town. In 2017, it was the first unit occupied in the revamped former railway station that was once where the town's supplies would be delivered. The buildings were brought back to life and have undergone a conversion to become a 200-metre terrace of restaurants and shops with an identical wooden frontage.

The impressively stocked shop appears to be a successful spot that offers wine tastings and sells a wide range of still and fortified wines. Before coming to talk to us, the owner completes the sale of two bottles of port to some American tourists. He tells us that, although the market for port is still strong, much of the demand in his shop comes from overseas. As with sherry, port is often hidden away in darkened cupboards and brought out only for special occasions. It is generally kept for too long, he explains, and is often past its best before being consumed.

A couple of doors along from the wine shop is a fascinating restaurant, Aneto & Table. The owners opened it in order to promote their wine, and they are clearly doing an excellent job of that. The Aneto family business was set up in 2001 by Francisco Montenegro and his wife Sylvia. He learned the winemaker's skill at the University of Vila Real and spent a decade fine-tuning various aspects of the trade while working for others. With that experience behind him, the couple bought a vineyard at Malvedos-Pinhão in the Douro and set about making table wine. The first year's production was 5,000 bottles of red and this has grown each year to encompass different types of wine including white, rosé and sparkling.

They now grow vines in three parts of the region and there are thirteen Aneto wines with an annual output of around 60,000 bottles. When I contact Francisco later, he explains that roughly half of that number finds its way into export markets, mainly in European countries such as Germany, Switzerland, Belgium and the Netherlands. The rest is consumed in Portugal, and the restaurant is a way to attract new customers in both foreign and domestic markets.

Fortunately, Caroline had the foresight to book a table, as the place is packed when we arrive. Its point of difference is that instead of choosing wines that are a favourable match for food, as is typically the case, Aneto has created dishes that are specifically designed to bring out the best in Francisco's wine.

During our meal and a subsequent tasting in the adjoining shop, we sample some of what is on offer. We enjoy the sparkling wine made from Pinot Noir grapes while we scan the detailed menu, which gives greater prominence to the wine than to the cuisine, with brief notes explaining why the associated dish is a good match. So, a white Grand Reserva brings minerality and acidity that complements salmon in a pistachio crust with its accompaniments, while white Reserva enhances the flavours of half-cured cod served alongside a range of vegetables with differing textures. Sylvia is a hands-on boss and she takes our order, making recommendations that we are happy to follow.

I notice that Francisco's Reserva Tinto red combines Touriga Franca, Touriga Nacional and Tinto Roriz. Those same grapes are also used to make port. However, the process is completely different. Port makers combine them to create a base to which spirit is added before the fermentation continues. Aneto's Reserva Tinto 2018 is another proposition entirely. It is rich and fruity and a good example of why the still wine from here is growing in popularity. Everything we taste is excellent and there are several contenders for a place in my case. However, the red is typical of the area and the way the three grape varieties are used to make a wine that differs so much from port underlines the winemaker's skills. This is my latest choice.

We take the train back to Porto. Here, the big port houses dominate the riverside cityscape. Buildings bearing the names of major producers abound in the Vila Nova de Gaia district, and tourists shuffle round them for tours and tastings. It is still a buoyant industry and that is good news for its many employees and the tourism spin-offs that it delivers. For me, however, the story of Portuguese wine is the change in production levels and quality among makers of the non-fortified style.

Before we leave for home, we visit Porto's World of Wine, a fabulous museum that tells the story of Portuguese wine from virtually every angle, spanning soils, grape varieties, processes, and ending with a lesson in how to taste, then rounding off with a glass of port.

My aim when I started this project was to learn about wine from around Europe. My experience in Portugal has certainly been educational. I will keep an eye on how its wine industry evolves from here. In terms of the run, the heat and my limited fitness ruled out what I had hoped might be a decent performance. My experience of the race has also taught me a few lessons, not least the importance of applying sunblock when the forecast is for temperatures to soar.

Glass half-full moment: Realising how the standard of Portuguese table wines is evolving

Glass half-empty moment: Negotiating the final few miles

Wine selected for Colin's Case: Aneto Reserva Tinto 2018

(Postscript: On my return home, I learned that, tragically, the girl I saw receiving CPR – a 29-year-old sports teacher and gym owner – died in hospital three days later.)

Nine

FRANCE

TUNE OF THE DAY:
'Games Without Frontiers' – Peter Gabriel

In the days before electronic games, there was a popular puzzle composed of a frame containing sixteen spaces – four wide and four high – and fifteen numbered slates. The idea was to position the slates in numerical order by sliding them into the free space. To accommodate each move, another slate had to be repositioned. That is how my racing schedule has evolved. The plan to have twelve races in twelve different countries means that each change has a consequence for another part of the plan. So, choosing Portugal in May means moving Austria to another spot in the calendar and that causes a change to my plans for France.

The original idea was to enter the Marathon du Médoc in Bordeaux. It takes place in September. This is the grand cru of wine runs, attracting 8,500 eager participants each year. Typically, around 30,000 people want to enter the race. They sit, fingers poised, on the day entries open, primed for a task that is every bit as demanding as covering twenty-six miles of sun-baked tarmac – to secure a coveted place on the starting line.

The race was cancelled in two successive years because of the Covid pandemic. Each announcement ratcheted up the levels of demand for a spot the following year, making the battle for a berth even more intense as runners disappointed by the cancellations were guaranteed a place in one of the next three editions of the race. Holding off in the hope of grabbing an entry would have meant jeopardising my chances of bagging a slot in an event elsewhere. Hence, the puzzle analogy and my decision to seek a different French adventure rather than hope to get into Bordeaux.

With events around the country already luring wine-loving athletes, and continuing to grow in popularity, France is well-endowed. The possibilities incorporate popular winemaking spots including Burgundy, Beaujolais, Champagne and Provence.

These races are modern inventions, although as I heard during the tasting at Denbies in Surrey, wine running is an exercise that was created to ensure the fitness of vineyard workers as the harvest approached. I discovered what appears to be confirmation of this when, in the build-up to my French foray, I read of the Marquis Melchior de Polignac, owner of Pommery Champagne in Reims at the start of the twentieth century. He was a member of the International Olympic Committee and encouraged his workforce to play sport. He worked with Baron Pierre de Coubertin – creator of the modern Olympics – and the French president, Raymond Poincaré, to build France's first school of physical education in 1913. The idea was to have a training centre for French athletes as they prepared for the 1916 Olympics – an event that was ultimately cancelled because of the First World War.

Champagne would be an attractive destination for me, but it is timing rather than geography that drives my plan. With September now allocated to a marathon in Austria, I turn to the options for June. Le Marathon du Vignoble d'Alsace stands out for several reasons. It is an established event, has a choice of distances and appears not to take itself too seriously, with organisers dubbing it 'Le Plus Festif', in recognition of the focus on a day of fun.

This seems like another opportunity to test myself over the half-marathon distance. However, by the time I decide that this will be my French destination, it is too late and the race is full. That leaves a marathon or ten kilometres. I am not yet ready for the former, so the decision is made.

As a committed Francophile, I have been a regular cross-Channel visitor for more than three decades, sometimes managing several trips in a year for work and pleasure. I have been to most corners of the country, but not to Alsace, part of the Grand Est region that was formed in 2016 following a redrawing of France's administrations.

It is an area that has passed back and forth between French and German ownership over the centuries. I can only surmise that there must be something worth fighting for.

Unsurprisingly, it has been the subject of many detailed studies, eloquent words and entrenched views among eminent historians and academics over the years, so there is little I can say about its often violent past that has not been stated by others more knowledgeable than me.

In trying to educate myself a little, I have come across an instructive book, *Wine and War* by Don & Petie Kladstrup, which neatly encapsulates the seemingly perpetual struggles in a straightforward manner and shows how innocent people were drawn into conflict against their will. The book considers the impact of the Second World War on the winemaking industry, specifically Bordeaux, Burgundy and Champagne, as well as analysing events in Alsace, where the Kladstrups focus on the experiences of the Hugel winemaking family.

Alsace, which borders Germany and Switzerland, was French from the late seventeenth century onwards. However, between 1870 and 1945, ownership passed to Germany, to France, to Germany, and back to France.

The Hugels, who still run the family vineyard in the town of Riquewihr, endured each of those changes. They have been in business since 1639, meaning that celebrations to mark three centuries of winemaking were well into the planning phase when war was declared in 1939.

The book explains the personal impact of that latest upheaval on Emile Hugel, who was born French in 1869. Two years later he became German after the Franco-Prussian war, before resuming his French nationality at the end of the First World War in 1918. Germany annexed Alsace once more in 1940, and when he died in 1950 at the age of ninety-one, he was back to being a Frenchman.

The Hugels faced the grim reality of the region's constant state of flux, with brothers Georges and Johnny unknowingly fighting each other after one was drafted into the German army and the other chose to defend France. There must be many such stories, and winemakers are surely not alone in having suffered at the hands of invaders who often destroyed or stole all that they had toiled to produce. That is thankfully in the past, although the region's location on the border is reflected in the names of many towns and families, which have a strong German accent.

Places are commonly also listed in French and Alsatian – the main street in Dorlisheim, where I will be staying, is Grand' Rue but the sign also has it as Langstross, while some people, particularly those who are older, communicate in the local dialect. There are also sporadic examples of low-level graffiti promoting independence for the region, although that movement appears to have limited momentum.

The war destroyed families and their property, encouraging collaboration with or violence against the enemy by people who were not naturally inclined towards those behaviours. Many winemakers met their death, others would never recover from the tribulations they faced. However, there was one development that delivered a positive outcome and continues to do so. Growers in Alsace had been encouraged to plant high-yield but inferior vines following the Franco-Prussian war in the late nineteenth century. The French government had sought to change that focus on volume towards higher-quality native grape varieties after the First World War, but financial constraints had proved a deterrent to the growers.

When Alsace came under German control in 1940, the new regime applied pressure to make the change. In the face of resistance from the Alsatian winemakers, members of the Hitler Youth were despatched to vineyards across the region to cut down the vines. That meant there was a need for replanting after hostilities ended. Fortunately, the French government was generous with funding for the replanting. That enforced upgrade is still paying dividends, with the wines continuing to improve and the range of choices constantly evolving.

These days, wine tourism is a big deal. La Route des Vins d'Alsace covers around 100 miles and wends its way through enchanting landscape peppered with castles and other points of interest, passing between vines and vineyards where proud owners are eager to offer a chance to learn about the art of winemaking and an opportunity to taste some of their produce. Itineraries also exist for two-wheeled travellers and walkers.

The quickest way for me to travel to my destination is by train. The vaunted TGV (Train à grande vitesse) from Paris glides effortlessly through the verdant countryside heading east. Passengers can follow its progress on an app that shows we are rattling along around 190 miles per hour for most of the journey. Given that speed and the price of fuel for car drivers, it's little wonder that numbers of rail travellers have boomed in the post-Covid period and most trains are completely sold out. That was certainly the case for each of my journeys – indeed I was unable to book my first choice in either direction.

The service is smooth and reliable, helped by the fact that there are only two stops on the scheduled journey to Strasbourg (there are none on the return leg). The train's efficiency means we outstrip even the most aggressive drivers on the motorways that run parallel to the railway tracks for much of the journey. Even the fabled Bugatti cars made in the town to which I am heading would struggle to keep up.

Fields of mixed crops pass in a blur and church spires peer above the trees, betraying the location of the villages they serve. Traditional agriculture in the shape of drying hay bales, which are a nod to the recent arid spell, swaps places on the landscape with wind farms, before a more typical picture emerges as animals go blithely about their day in splendid isolation. Only the occasional marks of a tractor's wheels suggest any human existence.

We roll into Strasbourg in under two hours. From there it is a short hop to Dorlisheim, my base for the next few days and the location for the start of my next race.

The Marathon des Vignobles d'Alsace was first contested in 2005, and has become a fixture on the racing calendar among athletes and fun runners. This year's event has attracted record numbers, with around 5,000 going to the start line in the various distances.

After almost two decades of fine-tuning, organisers have established an effective set-up that involves a different starting point for the half-marathon, while the other distances begin at the same spot but with an hour gap between the two races. That necessitates a comprehensive shuttle bus service that flits between the venues throughout the day, transporting competitors and their bags.

My event will take the long way round from Dorlisheim to Molsheim, which is the adjoining town and home to the marathon village where registration takes place, stalls are set up selling food, drink and sports kit, and activities are offered to keep children amused.

Molsheim is a much bigger town than Dorlisheim. It is giving off a prosperous ambiance as I arrive there having followed the cycle path that runs parallel to the main road, passing the factory where the Chiron model is made under the esteemed name of Bugatti. In addition to being a large employer, the family owns a large chunk of the real estate in this part of the world, and its earlier generations, including the company founder, Ettore, are buried in the town's cemetery, where the family graves are embellished by a mark of homage from the British Bugatti Owners Club. Schools, colleges and a host of streets also bear the Bugatti name.

It has taken me a little longer than planned to cover the couple of miles to the race headquarters following an unplanned deviation as I headed along the main street of Dorlisheim. The higher level of activity on a Saturday – cars and pedestrians were out in number – suggested a population that uses the weekend to catch up on domestic chores. Some dart from baker to butcher or buy fruit from the stalls set up outside the growers' homes. Others visit the town's hairdressers or beauty salon, or possibly consider upgrading their bikes at one of the two shops that ensure everyone on two wheels is properly equipped, whether they are high-level competitors or casual riders looking to profit from the excellent network of paths.

Almost all of the commercial activity happens here, although there are two modern developments that have added chain retail outlets, restaurants and a cinema. Dorlisheim takes pride in its appearance, with the sign at the entrance to the town showing that it has been accorded 'villes et villages fleuris' status as evidence of its efforts to deliver attractive surroundings for its residents. The council has also implemented measures aimed at helping the environment, and drivers passing through between the hours of 11.30pm and 5am will do so in darkness, as streetlights and other public illuminations are switched off during that time.

As with most towns and villages in Alsace, the architecture has a strong Germanic flavour, dominated by brightly decorated, half-timbered houses. My progress feels more as if I am leafing through the pages of a wine list dedicated to local producers than strolling towards the registration point. Having followed recent social media posts by the race organisers, I spot some of the names of sponsors who will be providing refreshments on the course. Camille Panzer, Jacques and Christophe Lindenlaub, Sylvie Silberzahn and Francis Backert are among those that have sparked a flicker of recognition.

I am tallying up the number of signs identifying the homes of those keen to advertise their status as growers and winemakers, and to invite passers-by to taste – and hopefully buy – the fruits of their labours, when I am drawn by the sound of laughter to a courtyard belonging to the Domaine Pierre and Frédéric Becht winery. Curiosity steers me away from the street and I see a large gathering that appears to be a bunch of people preparing for a tasting. I approach the group, which seems to be made up of friends, who are chatting noisily and punctuating the conversation with peals of laughter. They are of mixed age, but with a dress sense that marks them out as runners.

A glance towards the compact but ergonomically efficient tasting room shows that it a sampling is taking place, so I ease my way inside for closer investigation. On one side of the room is a wooden semi-circular bar littered with open bottles. The tasters are pointing enthusiastically at names on the list of available wines and asking for samples. Local grape varieties and combinations of styles mean there are many choices when it comes to deciding what to try.

The Becht business is a real family affair, which is now in the hands of its fourth generation, meaning it has switched nationality in the not-too-distant past. Today, while Pierre Becht is the charismatic host dispensing the drinks at the bar, his wife, Christa, and son, Frédéric, stand on the opposite side of the room, taking orders and processing payments from the many buyers. Meanwhile, a girl in the warehouse, which is visible from the tasting room, is receiving and packaging the orders at the pace of someone who is thoroughly practiced in the efficiencies that are essential to keep things moving.

I join the throng and pick a couple of wines I would like to try. The first is Edelzwicker, which is made using a combination of three grapes. It is fresh, flowery, straightforward and easy to drink. I am sure there will be others with stronger claims for a place in my case, but this is a good start, and the Bechts sell a bottle of it for less than the price of a glass of plonk at home.

However, Pierre is not stinting in pulling out some of the good stuff, and I join a few others who are clearly knowledgeable about their Alsatian wines in asking to try a Riesling. This one, the Christine 2015, is an award-winning white wine from one of the family's two vineyards. It is sumptuous, full-bodied and just on the right side of sweet for my palate. I notice that one of the accolades the wine has secured is a gold medal in the Féminalise World Wine Competition, which was set up to reflect the importance of women in the wine world and which has an all-female judging panel.

The Christine is named after Frédéric's wife. He explains that this wine was first produced in 2005, and was his gift to her on their wedding day two years later. Since then, he has made it almost every year. It is normally fairly dry, but the 2015 is a little sweeter. The Bechts recommend it to wash down dishes such as scallops and those that contain citrus fruit.

Pierre moves a little off-piste when he cracks open a bottle of eau-de-vie – a spirit made from a range of fruit harvested from his orchards. He insists that a drop of the hard stuff will improve even his sparkling rosé, and there are plenty of takers among the athletes. I opt out, preferring to succumb to his forceful insistence that I try the red he is waving at me.

It turns out to be an excellent Pinot Noir, a grape variety that is gathering momentum in the region. Indeed, the Alsace testing commission, which oversees standards, announced in 2022 that it was admitting two red wines to its grand cru appellation, the highest level in its grading system and a categorisation that has previously only been given to whites. More are expected to follow in achieving that status as makers broaden their portfolios and the overall standard of reds improves. The wine in my glass seems to me to have all the essential attributes, but then I would not profess to know what the requirements are.

One of the group of tasters is ostensibly in charge of proceedings. He pulls a folder from his bag, confirming that the people currently in full tasting mode are competitors in the races. It contains maps for each event. A female marathon runner is particularly interested. She announces that she is looking to finish in three-and-a-half to four hours. Perhaps the eau-de-vie she is knocking back freely will propel her towards achieving her target.

It is early in my Alsace adventure, and the unscheduled tasting has given me a glimpse into the region's wine varieties. Although I had planned to do some sampling after the race, I think I have already uncovered the wine I want to add to my case. It also meets my criterion of being relevant, as the Bechts' wine will be served at one of the feeding stops during the race. I buy the Christine.

I now need to pop back to the hotel to deposit my vinous loot before heading into Molsheim. I discover that the path I was following when I stumbled upon the Bechts' tasting room was the long way round – serendipity indeed.

This time I follow the direct route to the Hotel de La Monnaie, which is race headquarters for the weekend. It is a former mint that has had several uses since the French Revolution and is now owned by the local authority. I pick up my number and, with the formalities complete, I can now focus on the run.

Race day starts with a gentle stroll to the start, close to my hotel. The venue is the car park of the Cora Supermarket, which is closed today. I arrive more than half an hour before the event to experience the pre-race atmosphere. The place is a hive of activity. A bus is standing by to take those entered for the half-marathon to their starting point, and those in my race are warming up.

I am struck by the number of people in fancy dress, clearly buying into the 'festif' description. There are two Braveheart characters, resplendent in their kilts, numerous Smurfs, a few people in non-descript combos and enough superheroes to ensure that nothing can possibly go wrong today. Judging by the finger pointing and chat behind cupped hands, some people are puzzled by the guy who is not part of a group and has turned up in a luminous pink bikini and top-of-the-range running shoes, not least by where he plans to pin his race number.

Tutus and wigs are everywhere, worn almost exclusively by males, while some Vikings appear to have made the trip from Sweden. An American sitting on the ground in front of me groans when, in a font size that is visible to all of those close by, he receives a text informing him that his running buddy has been forced to call off.

Top honours for commitment go to the wedding party, who look as if they have just come from the church. The groom's shorts – nattily partnered with a shirt, bow tie and dark jacket – are the only concession to the fact that he is about to run through vines via a network of gravel paths and farmland. There is no such allowance for the bride or her two bridesmaids other than the practical footwear they have wisely donned for the occasion.

One runner, who may be a local with a German name rather than someone who has made the cross-border trip, is warming up with what appears to be excessive vigour. He is a man of similar age to me, and the sprinting forwards and in reverse – an impressive skill but one I hope will not be required today – knee-raising and enthusiastic stretching suggest that he is expending more energy than is necessary in the final minutes before we get going.

The group forms at the start, with runners three or four abreast behind barriers that create a narrow space and mean it will take several minutes for more than 1,000 runners to cross the line after the starting countdown. Around ninety seconds behind the first to leave, I begin my run. There is much jostling for position and a girl in front of me is causing mayhem as she runs from left to right then back to the left seeking space. A man behind her shakes his head and extends his arm, ready to push her if she re-crosses his path. I am a little further back, but it is also busy here.

We cross the Dorlisheim-Strasbourg railway line and turn left towards the vine-packed hills that overlook the town. Roadside crowds cheer heartily as the throng thins out and the slower runners fall back. Despite the cramped space that means my halting progress is punctuated by stumbles, I chalk up the opening mile in reasonable shape.

The tarmac surface gives way to a stony farm path and we see a sign for the day's first feeding station. On offer is an array of wines and some sweet brioche for those who are in no hurry – the organisers call it a relais gastro-vinique. It's a little early in the day for me so I give it a miss. A subsequent article in the local newspaper will quote some critics who believe the twelve wine stops dotted around the marathon course are a reckless invitation that could prove damaging to the health of the runners. There are three wine stops in my race. No one I see is complaining. The organisers would also claim that they take the health of all competitors seriously. Indeed, they insist that everyone who enters produces a doctor's certificate confirming that competing in the race poses no apparent risks to their health. I'm not sure what my GP thought of my plan, but he signed me off as fit to make the trip.

The course is undulating rather than hilly at this stage, and things are generally going smoothly. Perhaps the two young volunteers from the state-run Protection Civile first aid organisation had expected more action, or maybe they are still recovering from last night. Either way, they are largely unmoved by what they see as the unremarkable group strides past.

As we approach the halfway point and the day's sharpest climb, a teenager at the side of the track using cowbells for encouragement decides to make himself heard and he also shouts a few words of support as the circuit kicks upwards.

The second wine-tasting stop offers a Pinot Blanc by the Becht family. However, while I now know a little more about this particular offering and would relish the chance to have another glass, accompanied, if I wish, by kugelhopf – the cake baked in a mould and a popular choice for breakfast in this region – I opt out. Having passed an earlier water stop, I feel it would be wise to take on some hydration and grab a cup. The race organisers place great emphasis on the environmental aspects surrounding the races, and runners are unable to take drinks beyond the short feeding zone. I manage to take on some fluid before depositing my cup, but thankfully the temperatures are little more than twenty degrees, so a few mouthfuls prove to be adequate.

We are now running through the vines that produce grapes for much of the wine that is made in the village. Some of it is available at the next feeding station. Again I decline, as do most of those ahead of me. Shortly afterwards, I catch and overtake the Braveheart boys. I suspect they are discovering that kilts are not the most aerodynamic sportswear.

The next hill is testing but less brutal than many I have encountered on my travels. The downward stretch takes us back onto tarmac and into the town of Mutzig, which I visited a couple of days ago. One of the race volunteers is standing at the roadside with a garden sprinkler set to manual mode, and he uses it to send jets of water at each of the passing runners.

I recognise my surroundings as we cross La Bruche canal and turn right along the bank, where a band has set up and is playing a slow, instrumental version of 'Are You Lonesome Tonight'. If my ears are not deceiving me, the tune combines an electric guitar and an accordion. Bizarrely, hearing the music gives me a lift and I produce my fastest mile so far.

Clearly the expectation was for warm weather as, shortly afterwards, another watering system has been rigged up and attached to a railing. It is spraying a fine mist that cools the system but is not as big a shock as the dousing we received earlier.

We pass through a park on the edge of Molsheim, where fathers stop playing with their children to lend their support to runners. The course dips slightly and stewards offer an enthusiastic reminder that we are almost finished.

Ahead, I see a man whose gait suggests he is tiring. I guess that he is a similar age to me, so I make him my target for the closing half-mile, believing that will move me up the results by a place. I catch him just before the final turn into the home stretch and maintain my momentum as I approach the finish.

A voice from the crowd shouts 'allez Colin', and I realise that he is reading the name printed on my number, rather than someone I know. I am moving freely and I accelerate once more to cross the line at a good pace, then question whether I had too much left in the tank at the end.

I have finished comfortably in the top quarter and I am sixth in my age category, so I am relatively happy. It has been a good test, just right for me in my current state of fitness. My Achilles has been grumbling but caused no real grief during the run. I collect my race T-shirt and finisher's bottle of wine, which has a special label marking the occasion, then head for the race headquarters. Part of the Hotel de La Monnaie has been transformed into a treatment room where local physio students are offering post-run massages. Seb asks a few questions about my Achilles problem and rubs it gently then suggests that I rest it and resume training carefully. As I stand up, I note that I have left a pool of sweat on the physio's bench, so a shower looks like a wise move and the excellent race logistics mean that making the trip to my hotel isn't too much of an effort. Before I do, I pop into the town centre to buy today's copy of the local newspaper, *Dernières Nouvelles d'Alsace*. Prominent among the sports pages is a report of the children's events, which form part of the overall weekend of racing and were contested in Molsheim twenty-four hours before the adult programme.

On my way to the shuttle bus, I pass the finishing line. The man with the elaborate preparation is completing his run. He punches the air in delight, clearly having accomplished his goal. Perhaps the warm-up worked for him, but I am convinced that he would have gone even quicker if he had eased off on his pre-race exertions.

I then catch a return shuttle to see the presentation to winners of the longer events. Stalls in the race village are doing a brisk trade. Many of the finishers have been reunited with friends and family, while some have laid out picnics and have already opened the Pinot Blanc they picked up at the finish.

That bottle is a nice reward for the morning's exertions, but a mere dribble compared to the haul of wine given to the male and female winners of the marathon. Among their prizes is a contribution equivalent to their weight from the local winemakers. This takes the form of a convoluted exercise involving some of those whose produce is about to be given away.

First comes Viola, winner of the women's race. She sits on a chair at one side of a giant set of scales. At the other is a wooden box into which the wine is placed bottle by bottle, with the announcer reporting enthusiastically as another is added until an equilibrium is established. The sponsor who is providing the award has the task of filling the box and he adds a few bottles of crémant, the sparkling wine that needs reinforced glass bottles to prevent explosions and therefore weighs a little more. Sixty-one bottles later, Viola rises into the air and the balance is achieved. Next up is local favourite, Laurent, a comfortable winner in the men's race, who, as reward for his success, will make the trip to his home a couple of miles away with seventy-six bottles seeking a place in his cellar.

The frivolities resume among those enjoying the light-hearted atmosphere of the day and the favourable conditions. I return to the hotel after dinner, having had another confirmatory glass of the excellent Becht wine that is in my suitcase, to find a crowd of marathon tourists in the outside bar.

They are enjoying the dying embers of the sun, feeling fortunate perhaps that the forecast storms failed to materialise and spoil their day. It is only a stay of execution, however, and a couple of hours later the meteorological mood takes a turn for the worse.

Thunderclaps hint at what is to come, and lightning illuminates the sky. Rain pours down and hailstones the size of marbles rattle off my bedroom window. I wake the following morning to flooded streets and see hotel guests checking their cars for hailstone-inflicted damage. I hope that this is not replicated among the vines that are the lifeblood of the winemakers who joined the running celebrations. It is a reminder of the capricious nature of their business that a single storm could have disastrous consequences for their harvest later in the year.

And so my French experience draws to a close. Alsace is an intriguing part of the country, and its proximity to Germany is evident in aspects of the culture, in addition to the names that adorn towns, streets and individuals. But it is unquestionably

France, and it seems that the current generation is happy for it to remain that way.

Glass half-full moment: Discovering an intriguing and historic area of France

Glass half-empty moment: Trying to negotiate the narrow starting funnel

Wine chosen for Colin's Case: Domaine Pierre and Frédéric Becht Riesling Christine 2015

Ten

HUNGARY

TUNE OF THE DAY:

'Dancing in the Dark' — Bruce Springsteen

The headtorch I am wearing is proof that this event is different from the others on my schedule. It is 10pm on Saturday evening, and, as the people of Budapest stroll along the banks of the Danube on their way to or from the bars and restaurants of the Hungarian capital, I have joined 400 or so runners at the spectacular Várkert Bazár for a race that forms part of an extensive programme of events over a variety of distances, with almost 4,000 competitors in total.

The neo-renaissance building, which overlooks the start, was completed in 1873 as an enclosure for the Buda Castle Garden. Originally, it housed shops, workshops and a gallery, but it was demolished after sustaining heavy damage during the Second World War. An ambitious and massively expensive restoration project began in 2013 and was completed the following year. It now serves as a cultural space that includes museums and restaurants, while offering an area to relax and stroll through the immaculately tended gardens. Tonight, resplendent in illuminated glory, it forms the start and finish for the Budapest Night Run.

Of all the countries I am visiting, Hungary arguably has the richest and most complex history. Human remains are said to have been discovered in the area from 350,000 BC. Since the first century AD, it has, at various times, come under the control of Romans, Magyars, Mongols, Turks and Habsburgs. The Austro-Hungarian Dual Monarchy was created in 1867 and endured until the First World War. The 1921 Treaty of Trianon caused Hungarian territory to shrink to just over one-quarter of its former size. Then, after co-operating with Hitler during the Second World War in exchange for the return of a large chunk of that lost land, Hungary was occupied by the Red Army and became a communist republic, a situation which lasted until 1989 when that regime crumbled and the Hungarian Republic was declared.

Since then, the country has opened up, joining NATO in 1999 and the European Union five years later. Hungary has not yet been accepted as a member of the euro and continues to use the forint. That said, I will discover during my visit that many shops and restaurants show prices in both currencies, although payment is normally in forints rather than euros.

Since taking charge of its destiny, Hungary has experienced various fiscal and social issues, and the government under Viktor Orbán has been particularly aggressive in its opposition to migrants from the Middle East and Africa. Economic growth was solid in the years before the Covid pandemic, and that positive trajectory should resume in the coming years provided the impact of demographics such as an ageing workforce can be overcome.

The landlocked nation has a population of around ten million, of which roughly one-fifth live in the capital, Budapest. The city enjoys legacies from various stages of its colourful history and is a UNESCO World Heritage site. It straddles the Danube and comprises two disparate parts, the hillier Buda area, which is dominated by the castle that watches over its people, and Pest, the flatter, livelier part on the opposite side of the river. The two came together in 1849 with the opening of the first of the eight bridges that now link them.

As a vibrant capital city with a rich cultural past, Budapest has a great deal to see. There is no way I can do it justice on my brief visit, but I want to get a flavour of the place and I am hoping to be convinced that it is worth a repeat trip at some point.

The 100E bus is an express service from the airport, stopping only twice as it whisks passengers into the city centre. After passing industrial works, it proceeds through anonymous suburbs featuring blocks of what look like communist-era flats where many of the city's working classes live. We then ease past the Ferencváros football stadium and MWM dome, Europe's largest handball arena, into the Budapest of the guidebooks, with tree-lined avenues framed by imposing buildings that serve a variety of purposes, from homes and offices to important addresses on the cultural landscape, such as the Hungarian National Museum. Behind its imposing colonnade is a rich collection of exhibits. The building is accessed by stairs where a runner is recreating the scene from *Rocky* by sprinting up and down the steps and measuring his performance on his stopwatch.

I belatedly realised that the run coincides with the weekend of the Hungarian Grand Prix, and the city will be awash with F1 fans. As I will discover when I follow my race day habit of buying a local newspaper, it also proves to be the big sporting story of the *Magyar Nemzet*, sharing the bulk of the back page coverage with tales of the city's football teams. The publication's pro-government bias is evident from stories about immigration and favourable reporting of Orbán.

Within a few minutes of stepping off the bus, I see a huge crowd gathered outside the Ritz-Carlton Hotel hoping to glimpse the motor racing stars who are staying there. I also see the ubiquitous orange of all Dutch sports supporters, here this weekend to provide backing for Max Verstappen as he bids to strengthen his challenge for the world title. Had I checked the calendar before making my arrangements, I could perhaps have made the weekend into a sporting double-header. At least I now know why travel and accommodation were so expensive.

My initial impression is of a city brimming with energy and character. The area around the river boasts wide streets and classic architecture, which strike me as being similar to some of those in central Paris. Construction projects are peppered across the landscape and cranes dominate sections of the skyline. Some of the work is the restoration of ancient structures, while new buildings are also emerging. Traditional shops survive but many lie empty and are in need of rescue. This is already underway in some pockets of the city, where younger members of the population are repurposing premises for twenty-first-century life. Cool cafés and edgy bars share space with trendy retail outlets and burgeoning businesses that seek to surf a wave of entrepreneurism that has emerged since communism was swept aside. International chains have a presence in the streets around Vörösmarty Square, but on my walk across the river from Pest to Buda, where my hotel is located, small businesses appear to be holding their own.

Budapest is best-known as a cultural city and in that regard its burnished glory is undimmed. Museums, churches, galleries and the unparalleled waterside neo-Gothic parliament building are awe-inspiring. It is easy to understand why advocates for visits to this history-steeped gem come back frequently for an update.

Round each corner is a commemorative sign, a statue or a noteworthy building. Edinburgh-born Adam Clark has a wall-mounted plaque explaining that he died before his projects could be completed. He was, nonetheless, an influential figure, as I will discover later. Another foreigner honoured by the city is Shakespeare.

Budapest is endowed with many other absorbing artefacts telling the stories of famous residents, politicians, sportspeople and actors. One name so revered that it features prominently in a range of settings is that of Ferenc (Franz) Liszt, the composer and musician. The city's airport, various sculptures, numerous educational establishments and a memorial museum are all dedicated to a man who was actually born in what is now

185

Austria and died in Germany, although it is claimed that he saw himself as a proud Hungarian.

I am captivated by the street art, although my lack of linguistic skills means the signs remain a difficult-to-decipher mix of hard consonants and unintelligible grammatical accents. That also means my efforts to communicate with locals in their language founder instantly, and I struggle to get beyond 'hello' and 'thanks'. Typically, of course, they speak excellent English, which is the common language among tourists from around Europe and beyond. One other word I have picked up is 'fejlámpa', meaning head light, and relevant for the run, which is number ten on my list of twelve.

Clearly, the race is only part of the reason for this trip. Against a backdrop of frequent change, evolution and revolution, one thing that has remained constant is Hungary's reputation as a wine country. Apparently, the Romans first brought vines to the area and, over the years, the country's winemakers have delivered a high-quality product, although standards slipped during the period of Soviet control, when much of the character of Hungarian wine was drowned in a sea of volume and homogenisation. Change for the better has taken place and the country now ranks seventh in Europe in terms of production volumes, with an output that is around one per cent of the global total.

There are seven wine-making regions, which sub-divide into twenty-two smaller areas scattered across the country. That clearly suggests a wide variety of styles and underlines the difficulty in trying to sketch a true picture of the Hungarian wine industry. Records show that native vines have been

186

augmented over the centuries by importing new varieties from elsewhere in Europe, while there is also a movement to bring back some of the ancient types that were lost under the communist regime. It has taken time to recover from the period of Soviet control, but the excellence of Hungarian wine has rocketed since 1990.

The two big hitters with an international reputation are Tokaj aszú and Bull's Blood. The first spans the full gamut of quality, with some poorer versions seeking to piggy-back on the top-of-the-range products, and I note that supermarkets selling across all the price points appear to charge ten times as much for a high-end bottle than for the cheaper counterparts. In addition to appealing to anyone who enjoys sweet wine, Tokaj's status in Hungary is assured as a result of it being name-checked in the national anthem, a global exclusive according to those who are knowledgeable about these things.

The Bull's Blood – or Egri Bikavér as it is known locally – may not feature in songs performed by patriots or football fans, but it does enjoy a mythical reputation. A folkloric tale tells of a battle during the eighteenth-century siege of Eger, a small city that sits in the shade of the Bükk Mountains around ninety minutes from Budapest. Legend has it that the soldiers drank red wine during the battle so thirstily that some of it dribbled down their chins. The enemy Ottoman troops saw it dripping from the Hungarians' beards, mistook it for blood and retreated in fear.

Grapes were formerly grown in Budapest and wine was made in the city, with the castle used for storage, but that ended many years ago. More recently, many of the leading wine merchants were Jews. A large number of these businesses ceased to exist in a darker phase of Hungarian history during the Second World War. Those who survived suffered afresh, alongside others across the country, when vineyards were nationalised under communist rule and broken into small plots.

The regime change, which started in 1989, meant the plots were sold to individuals, allowing a new group of winemakers to emerge and buy land from the state. The second generation of that cohort has taken the helm over recent years and Hungary is now producing exciting, innovative, top-notch wines. However, many of these businesses remain small in scale and are dotted across the country. Trying to visit them would involve a travel plan that requires more time than I have at my disposal. Fortunately, there are several tasting rooms and wine bars in Budapest, which address that with a mix of casual and more formal sessions.

One of those is Tasting Table, a small venue lurking in a basement down a side street near the Hungarian National Museum. The façade may be unassuming, but inside is the ideal venue to learn about Hungarian wines, taste a few and enjoy the company of like-minded others.

Down a few steps from street level, the room boasts a bar at one end and a bottle display at the other. This business is the brainchild of Gábor Bánfalvi. He honed his sommelier skills – and his immaculate English – while working in the US, then returned with a headful of ideas as well as an American wife, before setting out to promote Hungarian food and wine. He explains that he visits producers weekly, most of them small in scale, although some have a higher output and ambitions to match. He also tells me that he is a runner, whose achievements include completing the Wachau Marathon in Austria, an event that I have as the final event on my schedule. Before I can ask about that experience, other tasters begin to arrive.

Two tables are laid out for the session, although tonight only one is required. I am joined by three American couples and one pair from the Netherlands. Among the trans-Atlantic visitors is a film maker from Malibu who is scouting potential subjects for the next series of a travel show and believes that Gábor fits the bill.

Our tutor launches his preamble, which he delivers as we take a mouthful of the first wine. In addition to serving products from eight different suppliers spread across the country, Gábor has been loyal to local suppliers in his choice of the accompanying cheese and charcuterie, which will enhance the flavours as we sip our way through a glass of fizz, three whites and three reds before concluding with a sweet Tokaj.

Our first sample is a pink sparkling wine produced in the Balaton region, ninety minutes or so from Budapest, and created using the Kékfrankos grape, something I have tasted before under its Austrian name, Blaufränkisch (Kék and Blau both mean blue). A story, or perhaps a myth, associated with this wine recounts that the grape takes its name from Napoleonic times when occupying soldiers bought wine using 'blue francs', which had more purchasing power than the official currency and meant they could secure the best wines. The one we have in our glasses is made in the same way as champagne, and is a delicious way to start the tasting.

A break in proceedings while Gábor pours the whites is a chance to learn a little about those sitting around the table. For six of them, the tasting is largely an additional attraction on top of their plans to attend the Grand Prix, which is the main reason for their visit to the city. The chat is convivial and open, and we will have an opportunity to resume later when Gábor is topping up our glasses with the reds.

He launches into his commentary on the whites, starting with one that is unique to Hungary. Irsai Olivér is a grape variety that was invented by a scientist, Pál Kocsis, in 1930. He created it by combining several other types, and dedicated it to the son of a friend, who was a respected wine merchant. This is a product of Hungary's biggest wine region. It is aromatic and light. We follow that up with two others – the first from the Mátra region and made with Hárslevelű grapes, and the second from Tokaj using Kabar – which have less pronounced flavours but also go down well.

The reds are equally broad in their range. Anecdotes about the winemakers show that Gábor knows them personally. When it comes to the Kékfrankos from Szentesi winery, we learn that the owner, József Szentesi, was an early beneficiary of the post-communism land sales. He makes this wine in Nadap, a village with a population of around 500 in the Etyek-Buda region less than twenty miles from the capital.

Szentesi's decision to make wine was the realisation of a long-held ambition, but it was not his first business venture. He took advantage of rule relaxation to become one of Hungary's first entrepreneurs. Initially, he imported billiard tables and slot machines from the West and subsequently set up a workshop to manufacture them locally.

That provided the financial clout to pursue his winemaking dream. The first bottles were produced in his brother's car workshop around 2004. Within a decade, he had been named Hungarian winemaker of the year and he was on his way to producing a range of wines and replanting extinct grape varieties. He has continued to revive many of the traditional Hungarian vines that disappeared during the drive for blandness.

Szentesi is a real student of wine and, after reading up on the history, he visited the Pécs Research Institute, which had kept samples of some traditional vines. He used cuttings from those plants to slowly bring them back into production, and continues to champion Hungarian grape varieties, many of which have names I would find impossible to pronounce.

There are perhaps a couple of details in the story that are not entirely clear, such as how he bankrolled the original business, but it is nonetheless a great tale. The wine we are drinking, the 2019 vintage, is also delicious. It has flavours of cherry and plum, and Gábor suggests that it has great ageing potential.

A Bull's Blood made by a brother and sister team in the southern city of Szekszárd using a blend of five grapes follows, and we conclude the tasting of reds with a wine from Villány, Hungary's most southerly wine region close to the Croatian border.

As we round off an excellent tasting with a sweet Tokaj and what's left of the cheese, the conversation among the group resumes and some decide to buy a few bottles of the outstanding wines we have tasted. All have been excellent, but the Szentesi story seems to be the most typical of Hungary's wine evolution and this is the bottle I choose for my case.

I wouldn't normally schedule such a comprehensive wine tasting so close to the run, but the fact that it is a Saturday night race, and wine shops will be closed on Sunday, means I had no choice but to do the tasting on Friday. It has certainly been worthwhile, and I am confident that, with a full day to recover, it will not hinder my performance too much.

Typical summer temperatures in the high twenties centigrade would make a run through Budapest a sticky experience. The headlamp and the scheduled late start are clues that I have taken action to avoid such a scenario. A neon display showing that it is twenty-two degrees as I jog to the start confirms that my gamble has paid off, although I am still feeling the heat as I follow the sights and sounds to reach the starting point.

A downside of waiting for dark is that it has been a long day, which presented a string of dilemmas. I wanted to see as much as possible of a captivating city, but needed to rest my legs a little. I wanted to eat, but not too much and had to judge the timing carefully. I wanted to be at the waterside starting point, but not so early that I would be hanging around clock-watching.

In the end, I opt to set off around an hour before the race and reach the hub of activity around twenty minutes later. The earlier part of the programme is in full swing. The kids' races are done, the five kilometre event is finishing and the ten kilometre competitors are making their way along the quay behind the designated pacemakers who aim to ensure everyone has a chance of achieving their target time.

Next to get going is the half-marathon. Competitors are led in the warm-up by a high-energy individual before being despatched into the darkness. Although many of them will be running into Sunday, they are not equipped with the headgear adorning the next bunch in line for the music-backed warm-up routine that means we are fully prepared for the countdown as the clock ticks past ten. We are off.

Torches bob like an army of glow worms, although I am currently feeling more sluggish than worm-like – hopefully a temporary result of the late start rather than a sign of an impending struggle. The race covers a vehicle-free route that takes in some of the city's iconic sights. That allows runners to view the spectacular, illuminated scene from streets that normally suffer from the frustrating bottlenecks and traffic jams that pockmark all modern cities. But, even in an entirely safe environment and with no sun beating down, the seven and a bit kilometre run – just under five miles to me – which I have chosen for the novelty value of racing with a light strapped to my head, is still a decent test of endurance. The seemingly random distance is a result of our race following the same direction as the half-marathon, which will cover three laps. The circuit divides neatly into five stages of almost equal length – a section along the riverside, a similar distance back, a climb, a descent and a flat finishing straight.

I avoid the initial charge from the starting point in front of the Várkert Bazár. When I passed this way earlier in the day, a thunderstorm had interrupted the construction of promotional stalls either side of the straight leading to the finishing gantry that is illuminated by flashing adverts for the sponsors. That proved to be a passing storm and all is now fine.

The starter pack, which I collected from the race organiser's premises – a running and bike shop in an obscure part of town – included my headtorch. Any initial discomfort at having a light strapped to my head is soon forgotten and within a few seconds I am no longer conscious of it.

I am, however, aware that I inadvertently stood among the runners likely to be battling it out for the honours, so as we run along the tram tracks during the settling-in period, I allow a few quicker runners to pass. Others who have made the same mistake are already being overtaken, but the group includes a broad range of shapes and ages and there is a light-hearted mood as we settle into a steady pace.

We step over a kerb and cut through the part of town bearing the name of my fellow Scot Adam Clark (although in traditional Hungarian naming convention, he is referred to in these parts as Clark Ádám). He was a civil engineer involved in constructing the Széchenyi Chain Bridge, which was the first link between Buda and Pest, and is currently being upgraded. The square to which he lends his name will feature more than once on the race route.

We are now on the lower quayside and heading for Margaret Bridge, which is gleaming through the darkness. On the opposite bank of the Danube, the Parliament building is even more commanding in the night hours than it was in daylight.

The first mile passes at a steady if unspectacular pace, and I am starting to feel more fluent in my running. There is a breath of a cooling breeze as we turn just before the bridge. The pace remains even for the second mile as we retrace our steps, running towards a fluid mass of light coming from the torches of those still negotiating the opening stretch. Around me, there is little movement in race positions – I have not been passed in the second mile, nor have I overtaken anyone.

We reach the first of several refreshment stations. Although the light and sound around the circuit may suggest otherwise, the organisers have taken steps to limit the event's impact on the environment. Runners must bring their own reuseable cups, which they fill from a series of huge glass bottles containing water and other drinks set up at various points. I still feel fully hydrated, so pass without breaking my stride in order to maintain my momentum.

We leave the riverfront and, cheered by spectators, negotiate a roundabout that launches an uphill haul of almost a mile. We are heading towards Buda Castle by a winding road that combines with the steepness to make progress slow. Having seen a shuttle bus and a funicular transport tourists from river level to the castle earlier in the day, I know how much climbing lies ahead.

Runners contesting the half-marathon started before us, and the leaders are now on their second lap. They power their way up the hill. I and those around me from the headtorch race can only watch in awe. A couple of drinkers emerge from a bar halfway up the hill to offer encouragement as I continue my struggle with gravity, and there is relief when we crest the hill and begin the downward stretch.

The road back towards the river also corkscrews around several bends and for a moment there is no one within torchlit distance. The temporary solitude is emphasised by the virtual silence, which is broken only by the chirruping of crickets and the slap of unseen feet on the tarmac behind me. This is proving to be a test for my grumbling Achilles. Shortly before leaving home I had a session with Rory, a physio who helped me in the past but has not been around over the summer because of commitments to professional footballers. The close season allowed me to draw on his expertise to ease the problem. His handiwork has helped me achieve a couple of longer runs – something I desperately need, with my marathon date looming ever larger. He has given me some tips on managing the injury. Climbing was fine tonight, but there is some discomfort as I run downhill and I sense that I will be stiff tomorrow.

Descent complete, I hear the laboured breath of a pursuer drawing closer. She moves past, her face a picture of determination, but fails to press on and I become part of a four-strong group with her and two other runners who have been dangling a few paces ahead of me for several minutes.

We pass through the Buda Tunnel, where a loud crescendo is provided by a group of drummers, the noise echoing around the enclosed space. With the fourth mile now chalked up, we are close to home, and we emerge onto Clark Ádám Square, where a woman roaring into a megaphone is trying to separate headtorch runners from half-marathoners who are setting off for their next passage along the riverside. One of those in my group veers left and takes a few seconds to realise his mistake, meaning he will not participate in our final charge for the line.

The finishing straight lies to our right, a red carpet covering the cobbles, and is flanked by a crowd several thick behind the railings on either side. Bright lights and music herald our arrival. I am glad that I will not be paying Budapest city's electricity bill, but the sights and sounds provide the impetus to raise my pace to something resembling a sprint. I manage to move up a couple of places, overtaking the two runners who had been in my group over the closing stages, before crossing the line, overcome with fatigue and dripping with perspiration.

An apologetic email arrived earlier in the day, explaining that the customary finishers' medals would not be awarded at the finish. They were crafted in Poland and delivery was halted by a fire that meant the train bringing them to Budapest had been unable to complete its journey. That's not a big deal for me, but medals will be posted out at some future date, we are told.

There are, though, no such issues with the bottle of white wine that was also touted as a reward for those finishing within the designated time. It is thrust into my hand within seconds of me crossing the finishing line, together with a welcome cool drink that helps to spark my recovery.

That was a tough test considering the race was over a relatively short distance. I will later learn that my finishing position in the male category equals my age, so I am reasonably satisfied with that outcome and particularly with my strong finale. I sit on the grass to regain my composure, sweat lashing from every pore, and a few minutes later I watch the presentation. Those on the podium are quite a bit younger than my children, so perhaps it is not surprising that the old guy is taking a few extra minutes to recover.

As I retrace my steps to the hotel, I elicit a few quizzical looks from revellers in pavement bars who cast a second glance at the man in running kit with a race number attached and a bottle of Hungarian Chardonnay in his hand as he plods wearily by.

Sleep comes easier than I might have expected after such a demanding late-night activity, and the following day I am a little stiff, but still exhilarated.

Before I leave, I'm keen to learn a little more about how a Shakespeare statue came to be a feature of Hungary's capital city. I stroll around the Pest side of the river. A signpost near the parliament building directs curious visitors to the sculpture, which stands in front of Starbucks on a weather-worn plinth with text that has been partially erased by the elements. The statue, it transpires, is a copy of a piece created by a Hungarian-born Australian sculptor, Andor Meszaros, and erected in Ballarat, Australia.

I realise that I have been spending too much time on my own over recent months when I conjure a mental image of a chin-stroking Shakespeare at a window seat, quill poised over his parchment, seeking inspiration from the fast-flowing Danube and pondering whether another coffee might help to stimulate his creative juices – 'to be or not to be, latte's the question.'

It's definitely time to move on and I prepare to watch the Hungarian Grand Prix on television before travelling home with another race ticked off and one more city on my list of places to revisit in future.

Glass half-full moment: Racing after dark in an exciting destination

Glass half-empty moment: The long wait for a 10pm start

Wine selected for Colin's Case: Szentesi Winery, Kékfrankos 2019

Eleven

BELGIUM

TUNE OF THE DAY:
'Rolling on the River' — Tina Turner

The words 'fine wine' and 'Belgium' are rarely seen in the same sentence. Chips, chocolate and beer are the country's renowned attractions in food and drink. So that makes this trip all the more interesting.

One of my aims when I started to consider my racing schedule was to discover some of Europe's less well-known wine areas. Nowhere is that more relevant than here. I'm in Wallonia, the heartland of Belgian winemaking. Some people may not realise that such a thing exists. Until recently, I was one of them. I'm fascinated to read that the country has more than 100 vineyards. I'm equally excited by the prospect of sampling some of the wine made in this nation of around 11.5 million people, and to understand why its production is gathering momentum.

Over the centuries, Belgium has been controlled by Burgundian kings, the Spanish, Austrian Habsburgs and the French before a union with the Netherlands ended after a revolution in 1830 and ultimately led to independence. In modern times, the country has seen much political turmoil, and twice endured lengthy spells of having no government, the most recent episode concluding in 2020 after 652 days with no official administration, beating its own previous record by more than sixty days.

Wallonia is the largest of Belgium's three federal regions – Brussels and Flanders being the others – so it has a government, a parliament and separate laws. The regional capital is Namur, close to the centre of the country and a half-hour train journey from Dinant, which is the base for this visit.

Historically, working life in Wallonia depended to a large extent on coal mining and other heavy industries. Its reputation for dirty, smelly stuff tended to mean the area went unnoticed, particularly by tourists, who were more likely to gravitate towards multicultural Brussels or the Flemish coastal resorts and cities such as Antwerp, Ghent and Bruges, which had more obvious attractions.

Most of the mines went out of existence in the latter part of the twentieth century, dragging down the associated businesses. That exacerbated the difficulty of drawing in visitors, and has meant that Walloon wine – together with the picturesque scenery – has pretty much flown under the radar.

Apparently, there is evidence of the country now known as Belgium producing wine from as early as the eighth century. That long-standing tradition in the industry is confirmed by villages around the region with street names such as rue du Vigneron and impasse de Vigne, although winemaking largely petered out.

However, that is now changing and it is enjoying a renaissance. Although most of the output is consumed in its home market, Belgian wine is forcing its way onto the international scene with exports gathering pace. The better products carry the designation Appellation d'Origine Contrôlée (AOC) of Côtes de Sambre et Meuse or Appellation d'Origine Protégée (AOP – a general designation that aims to bring greater consistency across European wine-producing countries). The Belgian AOC sign of quality was created in 2004 and means that it is the world's smallest wine-producing country with such a definition.

The river Meuse flows through Dinant, helping to enhance growing conditions for winemakers in the area. Many of the grapes are familiar names, but there are some exceptions, and I'm hoping to learn where they fit into Belgian winemaking.

I am travelling with Mike. We have known each other for around forty years and have had some great times. He's easy company, which is important since we will be spending several days together rather than the few hours we normally have when we meet up. Mike played football to a decent level in his youth and only gave up completely a few years ago when injuries finally took their toll. He has remained fit by cycling and running, so will easily handle the challenge that lies ahead. As he is also keen on war history, he already has some knowledge of this part of Belgium and how it has been affected by conflict.

Dinant is a town of around 14,000 people. Despite being only seventy miles or so from Brussels, it sits a little off the beaten track, as our journey attests. The train from Charleroi rattles through countryside where factories break up the greenery of the forestry and fields. A change at Namur thirty minutes later marks the halfway stage and is followed by a more pleasant landscape, where agriculture appears to dominate and rail tracks criss-cross the network of rivers. There is also a town called Dave. I'm not sure how that translates into English, but in my mind it suggests we are travelling in a place of relaxed familiarity, and that impression continues as passengers are deposited in charming Dinant, which seems to offer plenty to keep visitors busy for a few days.

It is the birthplace of Adolphe Sax, inventor of the saxophone, and it has several other historical landmarks. It is also the home of Leffe Abbey, a place best-known to me for making strong beer, but no doubt with a far more cultured background than that. In addition, the town has a dark and depressing story to tell about a specific day – 23 August 1914 – which will recur during our visit.

There is no footbridge at the station, so we wait for a freight train to pass before cautiously traversing the tracks. The striking initial impression is of the saxophone's ubiquity in a quaint town which has colourful waterside buildings that mix tradition with modernity. That, we will discover, is a consequence of many original properties having been destroyed during wartime bombing.

I glimpse the first of many ornamental instruments in the station car park then catch sight of a mini version hanging above a house door. When it comes to garnering credit for being home to the saxophone's inventor, Dinant seems happy to blow its own trumpet, so to speak. Over the coming days, we will visit La Maison de Monsieur Sax in rue Sax in the Sax quarter of town. We'll also see small and large replicas, all manner of references to the instrument and we'll find out about his life, his bankruptcies and the fact that he died in poverty. We will even dine in a creperie serving a dessert that is shaped into a likeness of the instrument and find a bakery selling saxophone-shaped couques, the famously hard biscuit for which the town is famous. It comes in a range of shapes and sizes, seems reassuringly expensive and is surely a gift to the dental profession. Mr Sax is obviously important to Dinant. And for anyone unable to find his house, a series of brass footprints embedded into the pavement will show the way. His statue sits on a bench in front of the house, while inside is the story of the instrument he created and the impact it has had on music through the years.

Equally important to the town is the brewing industry. Typically, bars and restaurants offer a variety of beers running into double figures, while wine is restricted to a choice of red, white or rosé in many places. That said, some higher-end restaurants have extensive wine lists, several of which include local winemakers – a couple of names feature prominently and are clearly getting something right. Overall, though, it's little wonder that diners of all ages match food to beer – some of it boasting eyewatering strength, with double-digit alcohol by volume not uncommon – rather than selecting wine.

Prominent landmarks in Dinant recount an episode that dates back more than a century. During the First World War, the advancing German army attempted to pass through neutral Belgium on its way to France, and took over the citadel in Dinant. French soldiers regained control and then, on 23 August 1914, the town came under sustained attack. The

Germans blamed the Dinantais people for firing on soldiers and resorted to brutality to extract their violent retribution. Throughout Dinant are memories of the innocent people – around ten per cent of the town's population at that time – who were slaughtered. Memorials use straightforward, no-nonsense language to express the hatred of the barbaric invaders who committed the atrocities and ensure there are lasting reminders of the blood that was spilled.

Walking around the town, it is difficult not to be touched by the stories of those who met their death. A statue at Tschoffen Wall is in the exact place where 116 citizens were lined up and shot – a bunch of wilted flowers lies on the adjacent pavement as a reminder that the current generation still acknowledges the pain. Meanwhile, the Leffe area of town also has a reminder of the 43 souls who met their death in a hail of German bullets, and other plaques and memorials across Dinant are tributes to those who were shot and then burned. But the most harrowing of the structures recalling that murderous day is a memorial to the victims. It was inaugurated on 23 August 2014, the centenary of the killings, and has dimensions that add up to 674, the same tally as the number of townsfolk who were shot. It has text carved into a brass box, designed in a way that ensures sunlight projects the names of all who were cruelly killed, with coded inscriptions of lines and dots revealing their ages and showing that some victims were babies.

Among those injured in August 1914 was a young Frenchman, Charles de Gaulle, whose statue stands beside the bridge that now bears his name. It leads to Avenue Winston

Churchill and the Promenade. In these more peaceful times, both streets are populated by bars and restaurants, while a fleet of cruisers offering short sightseeing trips sits berthed nearby along the river Meuse.

The shopping sector lies one street back, parallel to the waterfront, and is notable for the absence of international chains, with only one supermarket interrupting the independent nature of the businesses, which include bakers, a bookshop and, naturally, a beer specialist with several hundred choices available to the thirsty customer.

Perched high above the town is the citadel. As it has done over the centuries, the fortress casts a watchful eye over the town from its dominant position, which can be reached via 408 thigh-burning steps or a less demanding cable car ride. References to the many fierce battles waged over the centuries make this worth a visit, if only to experience the disconcerting reconstruction of a destroyed First World War trench that plays havoc with the senses of discombobulated visitors.

In addition to its other landmarks, Dinant is home to Belgium's steepest hill, La Montagne de la Croix, a climb of just under a mile that has an average gradient of 9.9 per cent and is 23 per cent at its most testing. Running up this would be unwise on the eve of a race, but we walk it – just because it is there. We learn that our lungs are functioning effectively, and that augurs well for the challenge that lies ahead.

We have entered the shorter version of the Descente de la Lesse, a run that provides an opportunity to enjoy the Belgian countryside. The route has several challenging segments and passes beside the river Lesse, which is renowned for its great kayaking. I have checked out the profile and this race promises to be fun and testing.

Testing is also on our minds with regard to the local wine. Neither of us has sampled what Belgium has to offer, so we are fortunate that we have found someone who is keen to help us fill that void.

Le Château Bon Baron winery is one of the key players in Belgian winemaking and occupies two units on an industrial estate around three miles outside the town. This is where the grapes grown on vineyards in nearby Profondeville undergo the process that is helping Jeanette van der Steen increase her profile, despite breaking almost all the winemaking stereotypes of family tradition, established markets for the product and a proven record of transforming grapes into great wine.

The path to becoming a winemaker started out with tentative steps and in somewhat haphazard fashion for Jeanette. She and her husband Piotr Strszeszewski were based in her native Netherlands and were kept busy running a consultancy company that dominated every waking hour, as well as frequently interrupting their sleep. Their two sons urged them to ease back on the pace at which they were living their lives.

The couple had visited Dinant frequently and decided to buy a property in the area. They also purchased a plot of land in front of the house, primarily to ensure it did not become a building project that might block their view. With that transaction concluded, the next debate surrounded what to do with the land. The outcome was the decision to plant vines. It proved to be the catalyst for a new business proposition rather than the finishing touch to the couple's plans for a simpler life.

As her determination to succeed in her new career shows, Jeanette is a force of nature. She has sought guidance from a host of distinguished winemakers in France and Germany, begging for opportunities to learn from them, and also securing a three-week placement at a specialist laboratory that allowed her to gain an insight into the testing and analysis that informs the growth and harvesting of grapes.

We are in the lounge that adjoins the winery. The room is adorned with paintings and sculptures that exhibit Piotr's artistic talents. Jeanette summarises her back story – the busy lives, the desire for a slower pace, the purchase of a holiday home in Belgium that would be renamed Château Bon Baron after they discovered a slab bearing that title, the acquisition of a half-hectare plot in front of the property, and then the first grapes three years later.

Unsure what to do with the wine which that harvest yielded, Jeanette passed it around her new neighbours. One of them chose not to drink it and instead gave it to a restauranteur friend. He was sufficiently impressed to find a place on his wine list for Bon Baron. Things took off from there, and several other restaurants have followed, two of them boasting coveted Michelin stars. More vines have been planted at other sites, giving a total of seventeen hectares and no fewer than fourteen grape varieties. Jeanette worked with the Dutch Academy of Gastronomy to learn about matching cuisine and wine and now specialises in classic white wines, plus several high-end reds.

The extra output means the annual total is approaching 100,000 bottles. With markets largely closed during the Covid pandemic, Jeanette deployed typical resourcefulness to find new outlets and two of Belgium's largest supermarkets now stock specially blended product ranges.

Some Bon Baron wines have had their quality confirmed by earning the status of AOC de Sambre et Meuse, and some have also won prizes in major competitions, Jeanette explains, as she leads us to the other building and shows us where she applies her talents. It is still a learning cycle, and she experiments with small amounts until she strikes a balance between each of the elements essential to creating great wine and only then starts bottling.

We return to the tasting room, where she brings eight bottles from storage and fans them across the table. As she opens the wine, she explains a preference for corks over other forms of closure, suggesting that this is further corroboration of her focus on achieving a superior product. That quest for perfection is also behind the absence of pesticides, and the manual harvest, which is painstaking but essential. Sub-standard grapes are removed at that stage, while other important steps in the process include slow fermentation and ageing in new oak barrels.

The first wine she serves is a Pinot Gris, which tastes buttery and sweet. The spittoons on the table will be used, but not for this one. Nor are they required for the rosé that follows, the slightly more acidic Pinot Blanc or the Chardonnay, which is reminiscent of a good Burgundy.

Grape varieties appear on the front of the bottle, although the next, the first of several reds in Jeanette's line-up, is called

La Grande. That title is her creation to describe a blend of Gamaret, Garanoir and Pinot Noir grapes. The name was dreamed up during the pandemic and aims to convey the feelings generated by Covid, as well as to quantify how her love for and support of jazz music helped to bring some relief – she is a sponsor of orchestras and musical events.

The wine continues to flow, and she disappears briefly then brings back two different vintages of her Pinot Noir in order to emphasise the difference that can occur from year to year. These wines are Piotr's realm and this time the spittoons are called into use, simply because of the volume of wine rather than any problems with its taste.

The Acolon needs to be savoured in full. The limited production of grapes used in this wine, together with the benefits of ageing, give it an intensity and spiciness that makes it a perfect match for gamey meat or strong cheese. However, it is also delicious on its own. It is made using a blend that was created in Germany in the 1970s using Dornfelder and Lemberger grapes. Global warming means that those varieties now ripen earlier in the year in their original habitat, and the cooler Belgian climate is an ideal environment for them to thrive. Competition is stiff among the bottles now scattered over the tasting room table for the penultimate spot in my wine case, but this is the winner for me.

Jeanette is an inspiring woman. The notion of taking on a project that would allow her to ease off has failed to materialise, although she has no regrets. 'I love what I do,' she insists, but does admit that developing a business with the potential to become even larger was never her intention.

In addition to pouring so many wines, Jeanette is generous with her time. Three hours later, Mike and I set off on our return walk, weighed down by a few bottles and blown away by the relentless dynamism of this human whirlwind. It has been an absorbing experience to learn how a complete novice has repurposed her acumen to become an expert in an entirely new business.

Our focus now turns to the run. We start our Saturday with a leg-stretching jog alongside the clear waters of the Meuse and, after a day of strolling and learning about Dinant and its history, we head for the race headquarters to register. Work is underway to set up the podium, and volunteers are dispensing numbers, pins and travel advice.

Sunday begins with a short walk to catch the bus that will transport us to the start. Today's challenge covers twelve kilometres, with half of it on minor roads and towpaths, while the remainder will follow footpaths and forest tracks.

The day's main run, the twenty-one kilometre Top Lesse, has been a feature on the racing calendar for more than forty years and, according to the official website, carries a hefty prize fund of 10,000 euros. Alongside the local stars on the list of past winners are athletes from around the world including Kenyans – who hold the records for men and women – South Americans and others from elsewhere in Europe, including the Britons Mike Gratton, whose other achievements included winning the London Marathon and a Commonwealth Games medal, and Julia Downes, an international-class performer in cross-country and road races.

Her name also appears on the honours list for the shorter event, the Lesse Douce. Mike and I will be in the field for the latest edition of that contest. The word Douce, meaning soft, suggests that we have wimped out from the sterner challenge of the Top Lesse. That may be true but, having seen the course profile, I am under no illusions about the severity of the test that awaits.

With more than 1,000 runners contesting the two races, and many others registered for a hike that follows the same route, it takes several bus trips before all are deposited next to the rural railway station at Gendron-Celles, where the shorter event starts. Organisers have attempted to avoid any potential confusion by issuing different-coloured numbers for each race. One guy is still befuddled, it seems, as he steps off the bus and looks for some of the familiar faces he is expecting to see. However, the background colour on his number suggests he has travelled to the wrong start. It is too late to rectify the error, so he will line up with our group.

A guitarist and accordionist have set up in front of the local hotel, disturbing guests enjoying a restful Sunday morning with an unnecessarily enthusiastic soundtrack as runners jog and stretch. Having arrived on the first bus, Mike and I are fully warmed up when the gun fires and we ease into action. We are somewhere in the middle of the bunch and that ensures there is no risk of going off too fast. We cross a bridge and descend to river level.

The ground is firm but uneven and potholed, and that calls for a cautious approach. The first mile ticks past and the field begins to thin out a little, meaning we can start to enjoy the surroundings. To our right is the gently flowing Lesse, while the terrain ahead remains relatively flat.

The path narrows and we reach a slight incline then encounter some steps. The group slows to the pace of those at the front as we climb to a narrow bridge, which becomes even more of a squeeze when a couple of startled walkers are trapped by the rampaging runners desperate to reach the other side, where the path falls back to river level. A similar sequence of events follows when we climb another set of steps and find ourselves running within touching distance of a railway line. Thankfully it is Sunday morning and there are no signs of trains.

We bump down and return to the flatness of the Furfooz National Park, where the concertina of bodies stretches out again as runners recapture their own pace and a steward directs us towards an area protected from the sun by a canopy of trees. The temperature is forecast to rise to the mid-twenties and is already on an upward trajectory, so this shade is welcome. It is still rutted underfoot, and my stride is also far from smooth as I pick my way between bumps and boulders.

We are now approaching the halfway point, where a group of eager volunteers are poised to serve us with bottles of water. I am quickly reminded of my limited skills when it comes to combining drinking with running. My efforts are reminiscent of traumatised ex-military pilot Ted Striker's problem in the 1980s spoof film *Airplane*, when he is unable to find his mouth with a cup and pours the fluid over his face and clothes. However, I manage to hydrate sufficiently and get back to a full stride. Shortly afterwards, I realise that Mike has been more cautious in ensuring that he takes on some fluid, and he has slipped back a little.

On our right is the magisterial Château de Walzin, which commands an impressive site beside the rough-surfaced pathway. The wider spaces mean I can lift the pace a little. I'm now in a small group with a few runners ahead of us gradually drifting back into range. We reach the Pont à Lesse, a bridge that is five kilometres from the finish. Then, as we pass Pont St Jean, approaching three kilometres from the end, I decline the second offer of water in order to avoid any need to slow the pace, which is now at a fairly steady level. Refreshment comes shortly afterwards in the shape of a garden sprinkler mounted on a cane, with its jets directed towards the road where it can offer maximum relief.

A policeman has stopped the traffic and we cross the main road. A sign displays the name Beauraing, its arrowhead pointed at a steward who ensures we remain on track. I can't help thinking it's a bit harsh on him, and I am sure he is actually quite interesting.

The Lesse now joins its larger counterpart, the Meuse, and the run-in becomes flatter, albeit with a gentle headwind. A few potential obstacles remain – the water is one stumble away and the path is bumpy, with cobbles adding to the discomfort. However, I am now moving relatively freely and I chalk up my fastest mile. That allows me to gain another couple of places, and I then pass a teenager who is looking even more desperate to reach the finish than I am – a moral victory for the old-timers.

We pass the monolithic Rocher Bayard, a thirty-metre-high rock and a Dinant landmark, which, from my waterside location seems to pierce the cloudless sky as it signals just over one kilometre to go. The volume of the announcer's voice rises a couple of notches as the hubbub surrounding the finish edges closer. I have enough in the tank to overhaul two more runners then I pip an orange-clad Dutchman on the line.

I finish in reasonable form and a large screen displaying instant results shows that I am comfortably in the top half of the field and tenth in my age category. Some fruit and a bottle of water soon have me back in decent shape as I wait for Mike to arrive. His red T-shirt emerges around the final bend and he musters a sprint to cross the line in a small group. That effort leaves him breathless, which is not ideal timing as the high-spirited announcer picks out the foreigner for a few words. Mike does have linguistic skills, but they do not include talking to a Belgian in French while trying to regain his composure after a tough physical effort. The announcer manages a brief chat with the exhausted Scotsman who is more interested in taking on water than offering his thoughts. He politely answers the questions before grabbing sustenance and marvelling at his new-found fame.

With the job done, we return to our hotel, which is just a few steps from the finish and where guests on the terrace have been enjoying breakfast while observing the spectacle unfolding below them. A shower and change of clothes return us to tourist mode and we get back in time to see some of the finishers in the longer race shake their heads and mutter about the toughness of the circuit as they cross the line.

We head into town in search of lunch. Mike is now wearing his race souvenir T-shirt and that piques the attention of an elderly lady at an adjacent table. She asks us about the race and is knowledgeable about the event, also querying our performances and opinions of the course. She reveals that the man to her left is her husband, who was organiser of the inaugural Descente de la Lesse more than four decades ago. She describes the course he devised in some detail, including a tale of the part that involved ascending a rock with the aid of ropes. Her husband nods his confirmation of her version and a smile creases his face as he recalls a logjam of runners waiting to deploy their climbing skills. I congratulate him on creating an event that continues to thrive. He asks if we chose version one or version two, which is a more recent addition to the programme. I explain that we contested the latter. A few minutes later, the couple rise to leave, with the monsieur cheerily bidding us 'good afternoon' in English, although I suspect he is less impressed now that he knows we opted for the shorter run.

We head back to race headquarters to catch some of the presentation, which proves to be a lengthy process exacerbated perhaps by some of the winners drawing on the skills of local brewers to fuel their rehydration. We decide to wait until the following day before following their example, and a visit to the Leffe Brewery proves to be an excellent way to learn about the methods and traditions of making a beer that is available in virtually all of Dinant's bars and restaurants. The experience is delivered through multi-sensory technology and ends with a relaxed product sampling in the tranquil garden overlooking the town. I also learn that people fascinated by beer are known as zythologists.

Having only ever been to Belgium once before – a trip to watch the early stages of the Tour de France cycle race almost two decades ago – I didn't know what to expect. I'm impressed by Dinant, the friendliness of its people and the cultural experience, albeit some of it is harrowing.

The wine, too, is largely underappreciated, and I have little doubt that it will become better known if Jeanette van der Steen and her like have anything to do with it. And the run was superbly organised, over testing but picturesque terrain. From my perspective, it was also good to have company and to benefit from Mike's knowledge of the local history. The impression we leave with is overwhelmingly positive. Preconceived notions of 'boring Belgium' have certainly been dispelled.

My focus now switches to filling the sole remaining spot in my case of wine, and the most daunting running challenge on my list. It's the big one, and I have just under four weeks to prepare myself for the marathon.

Glass half-full moment: Meeting the human dynamo, winemaker Jeanette

Glass half- empty moment: Learning about the harrowing events of 1914

Wine selected for Colin's Case: Château Bon Baron Acolon 2017

Twelve

AUSTRIA

TUNE OF THE DAY:
'Keep on Running' — The Spencer Davis Group

This is the third version. There were Dunaj references in Slovakia, it was Duna in Hungary, and now, here in Austria, the Danube translates as Donau. The river will provide the backdrop for my final run, a chance to achieve a long-standing ambition and complete a marathon.

The train from Vienna eats up the ground, clocking speeds of up to 140 miles an hour as it passes rolling countryside and hurtles through tunnels. I have to change at St Pölten, leaving my neighbour, a civil servant apparently, to continue analysing spreadsheets issued by the Department of Economics and sending emails. I switch to a less plush train to complete the journey to my base for the next few days, Krems an der Donau.

The second leg of the trip takes little more than half an hour, but with each station we pass, the bustling Viennese cityscape disappears ever further into the distance. Crops here are in mid-harvest, tractors replace expensive cars and eventually the outlook is dominated by terraced vineyards and wineries in the final kilometres into Krems, which bills itself as the eastern gateway to the Wachau Valley. We cross the mighty Danube into Krems and I head for my hotel, which is ideally placed to explore the town, and close enough to ensure that I should be able to drag my tired legs from the finishing line of the Wachau Marathon, the grand climax to my racing programme.

The Wachau is a thirty-six kilometre valley studded with monasteries, castles, stone terraces and vines. This is a haven for tourists of all stripes. Walkers, cyclists, history buffs and wine lovers each have reasons to visit. And Krems sits at the heart of it all. It is a town steeped in history, crammed with architecture and traditions that tell the story of more than 1,000 years of civilisation. In 1975, it was awarded UNESCO World Heritage status.

The race is the main attraction, but the grapes grown in the hills above the town were also a major factor in my decision to make this the final run on my schedule and my first foray into marathon running. This has been wine territory for centuries and it specialises in dry whites, generally fairly light in alcohol and made from a range of grapes, primarily Riesling and Grüner Veltliner. Most Austrian wines have classifications that mirror those used in Germany, although some producers in the Wachau use their own categories – Steinfeder, Federspiel and Smaragd.

The German system falls into six tiers – Qualitätswein, Kabinett, Spatlese, Auslese, Beerenauslese and Trockenbeerenauslese – the latter being a term that, despite the verbal gymnastics it implies, simply means that this is a sweet wine made from grapes picked later than the standard harvest and affected by noble rot. It just sounds much more than that.

At first glance, Krems strikes me as a prosperous town, hardly surprising given the strength of the local wine and tourist industries. The cobbled pedestrian zone features shops that nod to a wealthy clientele, with offerings of furnishings, expensive kitchen equipment, hand-crafted leather goods and high-end clothing – including traditional Austrian dress. They jostle for attention with the cafés and bars that do their bit to support the local wine trade as drinkers take up positions outside and inside at all hours of the day for a coffee accompanied by something that plays to the Austrian tradition of cake craftsmanship, or perhaps a glass of something from a nearby winery. One wine bar appears to be the meeting point for the army of retired people who gather to discuss current issues and possibly argue over the politics of candidates in a forthcoming election.

The streets also reverberate to the multinational accents of tourists. I turn a corner and encounter one group of around thirty who are each plugged in to the commentary that accompanies their walking tour of Krems' cultural highlights, including historical buildings, such as the fifteenth-century Steiner Tor gate, which these days marks the perimeter of the pedestrian zone.

The town is known as an educational centre, with a university, a hospitality school and a wine college among the establishments. The international student population communicates in English, albeit not as a native tongue. Among the conversations I overhear are discussions between Belgians and Spaniards.

Adding in the smaller villages and towns nearby, Krems has a population of around 24,000. The main artery through the centre is the Ringstrasse, a wide thoroughfare bounded by a range of building types, including some in the Viennese style that was the inspiration when this road was built after walls around Krems were pulled down and the land drained in the nineteenth century.

The townsfolk appear to take pride in their community and their integrity is implicit. The streets are spotless, and plastic bags containing newspapers for sale hang from lampposts, with an attached honesty box for payment. Meanwhile, wall-mounted cigarette machines and sweet dispensers – a blast from my past – are untouched by vandalism, and a bout of graffiti on the bandstand in the Stadtpark is considered newsworthy by the local paper. Drivers and pedestrians also seem to respect laws, with traffic lights and crossings evidently scrupulously observed.

Adjoining Krems is Stein, which was a separate entity until 1305 when the two towns merged. Stein, which is the German word for stone, is more creative and lively, as shown by the Kunstmeile – Art Mile – a district that is home to several churches, galleries and museums, including the Karikaturmuseum, which is devoted to cartoons and satire.

Despite the relatively bohemian mood, this part of town is more traditional in layout, with a warren of cobbled lanes leading towards the river in one direction and the vines in the other. It clearly attracts international tourists, as signs are often in English. I assume one plaque attached to a wall was the product of an online translation engine rather than a comment on recreational activities when it announces that the spaces at the roadside are for 'Stoners Parking Only'.

Several of the paths in Stein form the Austrian stretch of the pilgrims' route, the Santiago de Compostela Way – der Österreichische Jakobsweg as this part is known locally. Vienna sits around 3,200 kilometres from the Spanish city that is the ultimate destination for those who follow the Way. Pilgrims undertaking the walk obtain a stamp marking their progress at churches along the route, and when they complete this section, at the Bürgerspitalkirche in the centre of Krems, they can visit the tourist office to collect a certificate that confirms the achievement.

For winemakers, this is the time of year when the workload is ratcheted up as the harvest takes over. I climb to where the vines are planted, high above Stein. From here I look down on the river, where a barge laden with cars is making its way upstream and a couple of speedboats carve patterns into the water as they pass. Up here, the only sounds are chirruping insects, the voices of some walkers further across the valley and the noises emanating from machinery used in the grape harvest.

The vine-filled horizon seems a fair representation of the mountain Austrian wine has had to climb over recent decades. Back in 1985, a hard-earned reputation for a consistently good product was destroyed when diethylene glycol (DEG) was discovered in bottles destined for Germany. The substance was being used to add body and sweetness to inferior wines, giving the impression that they were better than was actually the case. DEG has no place in wine – it is a component of anti-freeze.

The fall-out was dramatic and, as is often the case with such incidents, many good, honest Austrian winemakers were caught up in a scandal that was not of their making, but which threatened their livelihoods. However, there was a benefit for those who survived. The industry has now recovered and the standards surpass anything achieved before that episode. Indeed, some of the wines produced now stand comparison with those from anywhere else in Europe, and some currently lead the way in terms of quality and value for money. This is evidence of a remarkable recovery from a humiliating blow that could have sounded the death knell.

Before I get to explore that a little further, I have a race to run, and it's the most taxing yet. In truth, this is the first time I've genuinely questioned my plan. Although my performances in some of the others fell short of my aspirations, and there were a couple where I had concerns over my fitness, I knew I could cover the distance. In this case, that's less of a certainty.

With that in mind, and the injury issue that has dogged my training throughout the year, I have downgraded my expectations. Initially, I had hoped to record a time that would qualify as 'good for age', as defined by organisers of major races such as the London or Boston marathons. I have no plans to run another one soon, but achieving such a performance would be a little affirmation, like a wine earning the status of Appellation d'Origine Contrôlée or, as I'm in Austria, Qualitätswein. However, the full-on nature of my racing schedule has meant that the gap between events hasn't been long enough to allow me to shrug off the nagging injury or build the mileage in training to achieve that standard, which is below four hours. So, my target now is simply to finish the race, although I still hope my effort will deliver a respectable time.

I have entered the Wachau Marathon, which is strongly themed in keeping with this area's winemaking traditions. There is a little pun in the strapline. Einmalig is the German word for exceptional and, by adding a W at the start and copyrighting the term, the organisers are linking this exceptionalism with wine – or wein as it is in German. This marathon is Weinmalig.

I go to register on the eve of the race and work is underway to transform the town's main green space – Stadtpark, right next to the event headquarters – into a village featuring equipment exhibitions, bars, physios and a forest of mobile toilets with the splendid name 'Pipi Box'.

The big day dawns. With the race starting in more than three hours and likely to take me another four or so to complete, I head for the breakfast room at the hotel. It is heaving with bodies, many of them already in running kit. The girl at the next table is Petra according to her race number, and she is clearly raring to go, finishing off her preparation by attaching the timing chip to her shoe before disappearing.

I resist the bacon and eggs, but eat as much as I can reasonably digest before returning to my room to prepare. I have laid out my shoes, with chip attached, T-shirt with number pinned on, and sticking plaster for a little manoeuvre that involves covering my nipples in a bid to prevent a recurrence of the painful friction-related injury I suffered during a couple of recent long runs.

The local newspaper, *Die Niederösterreichischen Nachrichten*, which is published weekly, has a supplement with more information about the race than I really need to know. It is, nonetheless, interesting to learn of the link to charity, the location of refreshment stations and the fact that the official race wine has earned gold medals in two international competitions.

It has rained overnight and there is a light drizzle as I head for the bus station where a fleet of vehicles awaits. They will transfer runners to the start in Emmersdorf, just over twenty miles away. My reservation for the forty-five minute transfer was confirmed in my starter pack, meaning we arrive just under an hour before the race starts. Travelling by train is also a possibility, although the journey takes much longer, while those contesting the half-marathon can opt to travel by boat. That distance has attracted the largest field and the biggest names. Philimon Kipkorir Maritim and Teresiah Kwamboka Omosa will eventually take the honours in world-class times, maintaining the Kenyan stranglehold on the event.

Some bus passengers are keen to engage others with chat, while many sit silently, contemplating the challenge. The serious runners stick labels on their own bottles, which will be delivered to various refreshment points. Some competitors have made their own travel arrangements, and there is already much activity when the bus deposits us at the start.

Emmersdorf is a sleepy little place, especially on a Sunday morning, and it looks as if the whole village has mobilised to assist at the start. Some help police to block the road, others are hoisting an inflatable gantry bearing the name of a sponsor, and a few are firing up a barbecue – presumably for spectators rather than competitors.

The race follows part of the Romantikstraße, the route that covers the 380 kilometres from Vienna to Salzburg and passes stunning landscapes that sit on the banks of the Danube. It was looking a little less romantic earlier this morning when low cloud obscured much of the view during the bus trip, but the signs are a little more promising now.

The point-to-point nature of the course means the only way to get back to Krems is to run. Pacemakers are available to ensure athletes have the best possible opportunity of achieving their goals. For the marathon, there are three slots of three hours thirty, four hours or four hours thirty. My hope would be to achieve somewhere between the latter two, so I line up close enough to keep an eye on the quicker of the two pacers, while avoiding the temptation to try and stick with him and risk blowing up.

The first three miles cover a loop that heads further away from Krems before a slight descent offers the first glimpse of the majestic Danube and we head back towards the start line where the crowd is still offering support. I have gone through the first mile a second or two faster than my plan, but overall I'm moving along quite comfortably as we pass the inflated gantry where we started.

I'm surprised that the miles seem to be passing relatively quickly rather than dragging as I feared they might. It may have something to do with the fact that roadside boards mark each kilometre, while my watch beeps after every mile, so I'm constantly reminded of my progress.

We are running through rural settlements, where residents have made an admirable effort to showcase their villages and support the race. There are twelve refreshment points, manned by adults, ably assisted by a band of enthusiastic children who become increasingly keen to be the supplier of choice and voice their disappointment when their offering is rebuffed or the drink is taken from another child. I have decided that the risk of becoming dehydrated is too great, and my combined running and drinking skills are unreliable, so I will slow to a walk at each feeding point to ensure I take on water without spillages. At the first couple, I take only water and I have no trouble resuming my pace afterwards, although that may change later.

We are following the B3 road, which is closed to traffic, and the runners are spread out. A couple come past, travelling at pace and I wonder why they have taken so long to hit their stride. I then realise that they are the fresh athletes who have just taken over for the second leg of the marathon relay, which is incorporated into the solo event.

Back in my world, I am still moving reasonably comfortably, with two others for company. Walkers and cyclists stop their own activities to offer encouragement, and villagers also cheer us on our way. We haven't seen a great deal of the Danube so far, as we are running through an alley of trees, but when it does open out and the river becomes visible, I find myself wondering whether Strauss would describe its murkiness as blue if he were writing his celebratory musical piece today. The tune comes to mind and I fear that I may not be able to get the pom-pom pom-pom notes out of my head. A solution

227

soon materialises as we pass a fire station in one tiny village. These places are apparently run as voluntary services and one group of civic-minded souls offer their vociferous support, their voices drowned out only by a high-decibel soundtrack. If I'm not mistaken, it is 'Whiskey in the Jar' by Thin Lizzy, which shunts aside the gentle strains of Strauss.

The musical theme continues as we pass through Aggsbach-Markt, and round a bend to see a band, decked out in traditional regalia including shorts and feathered hats, lined up on the lawn in front of the fire station as if preparing for a team photo, while gently performing a typical Austrian melody.

I'm still churning out respectable times. At the next feeding station, I pair my water with a chunk of banana. It probably has nothing to with my nutritional change, but I then turn in two quicker miles that help me pass the midpoint in a time that is faster than I achieved in the Spanish and Portuguese half-marathons.

I am aware that progress could be derailed at any point and there is the familiar nagging from my foot, which occasionally tips over into a sharp pain. He may have been Greek, but I address Achilles with a couple of Anglo-Saxon words and hope the throbbing in my heel will not worsen. The flat profile is a big help. Rare deviations from the pancake-flat surface can barely be described as hills, and would register only as a minor bump on some of the courses I have experienced.

There is an odd sense of relief when Krems appears on the road signs. The fact that it is shown as being nineteen kilometres away does not deflate that particular bubble of optimism. Andreas eases past on my inside, going well and evidently talking to himself. We reach a bend in the Danube and he waves enthusiastically at someone who is on the balcony of a house on the far river bank. As he does so, I note that he is wearing an earpiece and was in fact speaking to someone he knew rather than suffering from mid-race delirium.

I decide to go a bit gung-ho and take banana and an energy drink at the next fuelling point, hoping that it may deliver another performance boost. The effect is positive, but the combo doesn't move the dial to the same extent as my previous experiment. I decide that further banana intake may lead to a Pipi Box visit, so I revert to a liquid only diet for the rest of the race.

Four youths have gathered at the roadside and are slurping bottles of beer. Their musical offering is 'Eye of the Tiger', a rousing tune by Survivor, with connotations of power and strength. It seems an inappropriate choice for the way I'm feeling right now, but we are passing through Joching, so maybe they are just having a laugh.

I'm still toddling along consistently and I find myself enjoying the run, rather than just enduring the challenge, but conscious that I am now approaching uncharted territory having never before covered more than twenty-two miles. People around me are suffering from cramp and various other ailments, and I know that I could also succumb at any moment. One runner pulls up suddenly and looks to be in pain, but he responds to my question over his well-being with a thumbs-up.

We enter the town of Dürnstein, which is watched over by a fairy-tale castle. There is a short loop of just under a mile before we re-join the road into Krems. This allows me to see those who are immediately ahead of me, and I note that Petra from breakfast is moving smoothly, a minute or so in front. The same is not true of Johann, whose face is etched with pain.

With just over three miles to go, I try to convince myself that the distance left is only equivalent to a parkrun. It doesn't really work. For a start, I have never been this knackered at the start of a parkrun. I respond to my own kidology by producing a couple of slower miles, although I haven't lost my momentum completely, and I am a little surprised to overhaul Petra shortly afterwards. I then recognise my surroundings. We are passing Stein, on the edge of Krems – I wonder what the parking is like for the Stoners today.

I now want to avoid slowing to a walk, and that is made easier by the roadside crowds offering encouragement. My timing chip beeps as I run past a group of people who have set up a stall at forty-one kilometres. This seems an odd spot to be taking an intermediate time, but I later find out from the newspaper supplement that these are volunteers and for each runner who passes this stage their charity receives a euro from one of the sponsors.

We pass along Ringstrasse and go round the perimeter of Stadtpark then finish along a carpeted home straight. The fatigue as I cross the line differs from what I have experienced previously. It is a dull ache in my legs rather than a muscular burn.

A young girl has landed the less-than-plumb job of handing out medals to sweaty finishers in various dilapidated states, and I try to avoid spoiling her day completely by perspiring over her, or worse. The overhead clock confirms what my watch has been telling me – I'm not too far short of the four-hour mark I had initially hoped to achieve. That is satisfying, and perhaps a little frustrating. On the plus side, my second half was only a couple of minutes slower than the first. I also could look at the time lost by walking at drinks stations, essential though it was. One point I note later when I am in analytical mode is that my stride was shorter than normal. My run comprised more than 40,000 steps and, had I maintained the stride pattern but added just a couple of centimetres to each one, I might have gone under four hours.

For now though, I need to get the body ticking over again. Water and energy drinks compensate for the hydration I missed by not stopping at the final two stations for fear of being unable to resume running. There is fruit, of course, and then there is the welcome sight of plum flan and cheesecake, so by the time I'm ready to walk gingerly back to the hotel, I am feeling human again.

Before I go, I see Petra, who is speaking on her mobile and looks happy with her effort, and Johann, who stumbles into the recovery space and appears to be in agony. He attracts the attention of first aiders, who watch for a few moments then evidently decide he is in no danger and leave him to his own routine.

As I make my way back towards the hotel, I encounter another runner heading in a different direction. Spying my race number, he acknowledges a kindred spirit, shouting, 'servus', the local version of 'hi'. I acknowledge his call but I'm not sure whether he is asking me, or whether he is commenting on his own state when he says, 'Abgeschlossen!' ('done') and draws an imaginary line in the air.

I shower and change then return to the park. I have just missed the presentations, but there is some good news as Johann is standing at a table sharing a cup of something and some chat with friends. He looks around ten years younger than he did when I last saw him.

I stroll through the streets looking for a place to rest my legs and have a coffee, as well as carrying out a recce for tonight's dinner. It's all a bit quieter than it was on Saturday morning when producers were kept busy at the street market. Wine, fruit and bread were bought and consumed on the spot to the accompaniment of the town band in full flow, while bars and cafés were already doing a roaring trade. Today, the shops are closed, as are many of the bars and restaurants. The few that do remain open are fairly quiet, and it's clear that Sunday is set aside for other purposes.

I dine early and enjoy a glass of the local wine. The tradition in Austria is that it is served as an achtel or a viertel – an eighth or a quarter of a litre respectively, meaning a glass is either 125 or 250 millilitres – and is generally accompanied by a glass of water.

There are numerous possibilities for where to further my wine education the day after the run, but I have chosen to visit Winzer Krems. This is a co-operative of winemakers that was among the sponsors for the marathon, and had a team of ten in the race, so I am making my own small contribution in recognition of their support.

Sandgrube 13 is one of the Winzer Krems sites and is the place where the winemaking takes place. The winery sits at the top of a hill not far from my hotel. Knowing that it will take longer than it should to hobble there, I set off with plenty of time to spare and arrive quarter of an hour early, allowing me to investigate the surroundings. I see plastic crates loaded with grapes being tipped into a hopper then crushed by a giant juice squeezer. As I wander around the perimeter of the yard where this is happening, a member of staff comes towards me. I'm guessing that I am breaching some safety protocol, or that this is out of bounds because what happens here is top secret. Instead, he summons me and points to where I should stand for a better view. It's all impressive stuff, and now I'm keen to learn more about the process that brings all this together.

Having met us in the reception, our guide leads the group of seven to the Hiata-Hütte, a watchman's hut, where some clever planning means a colleague has already poured us each a small glass of Grüner Veltliner, and ensured it is perfectly chilled. The guide encourages us to taste the wine as she explains the background to Winzer Krems, which has existed since 1938. There are a small number of vines here, but most of the grapes come from other sites, which are owned by around 900 growers. By using Sandgrube 13 to make the wine, they are spared the substantial financial outlays this would otherwise entail.

We move indoors to a room in which the floor displays an aerial map of the land around Krems. It is where the grapes processed here are grown, and the map also shows the boundary where the neighbouring Domäne Wachau co-operative takes over.

Our next stop is the cellar where old vintages are kept, and the guide plunges the room into darkness for a show of sounds and lights that is the imagined conversation between wines of the past. We then move back into the modern world, to the cellar room, where we enjoy a glass of Blauer Zweigelt – a fruity red that takes its name from an Austrian variety invented a century ago and now the most widely planted red grape. The room contains Austrian oak barrels and offers a view over the company's fermentation space and cellar. Beyond the cellar, an extension is currently under construction. It will eventually accelerate the bottling process.

We move on to a cinema and pick up a pair of 3D glasses that will allow us to experience life as it is for vineyard workers. We start with a scene from winter when little is happening in the snow-blanketed vines, before observing how the growing season evolves. There is also a glimpse of the resident wildlife. There's a sharp intake of breath when the effects of the glasses give the impression that a tractor is heading our way, and a fourth dimension is added to the experience with intermittent puffs of wind that offer a dusty whiff of the vineyard.

The next part of the visit takes us past a series of holograms illustrating how wine and food match, then into a room where we are served bread and a glass of Riesling, as the guide leads us through a chat on the current Winzer Krems products, which are displayed on the shelves.

And we conclude the tour in the shop – the sales manager's favourite part of the tour, according to our guide. Grüner

Veltliner is the predominant grape, representing around half of the Winzer Krems production, so that makes it the leading contender for the final spot in my case. Helping me to narrow the options further is the fact that the official wine of the Wachau Marathon is Edition Chremisa Grüner Veltliner 2021. It is categorised as Qualitätswein and takes its name from the ancient spelling of Krems. The company's blurb talks of a full-bodied wine that will accompany a variety of dishes. This is also described as a 'meditation wine', which sounds intriguing but refers, I believe, to the fact that it can also be enjoyed without food.

It was possible to order the wine when submitting my race entry. However, it is also here on the shelves, making the decision straightforward. I buy the wine that will complete my collection.

And so my adventure is over. As I walk to the station on my final morning, it is raining, just as it was when I arrived. It seems symbolic in some ways. I have come full circle, not only on my Austrian experience, but on the overall plan.

I'm fairly satisfied with this leg of the project, and there is an element of fulfilment in finally achieving that niggling goal of running a marathon. Maybe I left it too late in life, but I can now tick it off my to-do list.

Is it out of my system? Abgeschlossen? The thing is I'm convinced that by being injury-free, looking more closely at nutrition and targeting my preparations for a specific race, I could run faster, and possibly dip under four hours. Never say never. Running gets you that way, even at my modest level. And with sixty years on the clock.

Glass half-full moment: Completing my first marathon at the age of sixty

Glass half-empty moment: Leaving it so late in life to make my marathon debut

Wine selected for Colin's Case: Edition Chremisa Grüner Veltliner 2021 Qualitätswein from Winzer Krems

Epilogue

WARM-DOWN

I knew from the moment I decided to pursue this adventure that I would find it tough at many stages. I was ready for the tribulations I have faced over the year, if not completely anticipating the form they would take.

Overall, there have been far more highs than lows and I reach the finishing line glad that I embarked on the project. Some people may have thought I had lost the plot, others possibly didn't understand what I was trying to do. Thankfully, most could see it as the challenge it was, and were supportive.

As I cast a backward glance and sum up the experience, there are a few things that stand out. Away from the athletic challenge, I learned about the history and energy of Slovenia and its people, the traditions that ripple through Andalucia, and the ambitions of English winemakers. I discovered facts that would otherwise have eluded me – that despite its Italianate sounding name, Bugatti is French, that a Scotsman played a significant role in shaping Budapest's cityscape, and that the saxophone is a Belgian invention. I gained insights into national stereotypes that are less evident in tourist centres – among my discoveries was confirmation that Italians and Germans have a far better sense of humour than they are credited with.

I travelled to some places that I would never have chosen to visit as a tourist. I certainly didn't have Dorking on my must-see list, I didn't know where Košice was, there were no plans to visit Dinant or Dorlisheim, and Vidor wasn't on my radar.

I have learned a little more about wine and the honest, hardworking people who labour in fields and wineries to create a product that embodies their boundless passion. In some cases, I learned from vineyard staff, and in others I met the individuals who are proudly responsible for creating a product that bears their name. I came across some fabulous characters and I managed to uncover a few wines that would have remained tucked away in the darker recesses of specialist wine shops or obscure pages of arcane websites, far from my sphere of knowledge.

In addition, I had my eyes opened to a surfeit of information that at times is as difficult to swallow as a corked Chardonnay. The wine industry overflows with hyperbole. So many vineyards, wineries, bodegas and even countries claimed to be first, biggest, best, award-winning, traditional or ground-breaking that finding something without labels or grand titles was something of a rarity. I did my best to verify the accuracy of these claims, but acknowledge that it's sometimes impossible to confirm the absolute veracity. If anything in this book is wrong, then it is likely to be a mistake on my part, but it may also be the case that the error stemmed from a myth that was peddled by a guide or a winemaker intent on promoting their product.

I spent more time than I would have wished waiting for buses, trains and planes. That was a by-product of travelling to places that are not on the traditional tourist map but are the venues for wine-related races, or because I was doing so out of season. I also spent hours in border control queues – a non-negotiable requirement in these post-Brexit days – and my passport now contains an extensive collection of entry and exit stamps.

I was fortunate with the weather. There was driving snow in Italy, heavy rain in England, freezing mist in Germany, and a damaging hailstorm in France. But all of those meteorological episodes occurred either the day before or the day after the race. Budapest also showed its capacity for storms of biblical proportions, but fortunately that was on the morning of the run and by the time we lined up in the evening it was dry and warm, while rain in Austria cleared shortly before the race started. Clearly, I was lucky.

I went into this challenge knowing that the scope for things to go wrong was substantial. The need to be flexible over my schedule was always clear. I exacerbated the difficulty by insisting on a different country for each of my twelve runs and on completing one a month. The result was that selecting a race in one place because of convenient timing meant ruling out another in that same country, even when the second option may have been more attractive than the one that earned the nod.

The first three events I pencilled into my schedule were Bordeaux, Moldova and the German Wine Route. In the end I did none of these. Instead, my timetable evolved as I juggled with geography to ensure I didn't duplicate any destination. Fortunately, Spain, Italy and France offered plenty of choice, so that gave me flexibility, while the wonderful parkrun concept was a valuable tool when it came to filling blanks in my roster.

A marathon debut at the age of sixty was a source of some apprehension and therefore something I regard immodestly as a decent achievement and a long-standing ambition realised. The time I recorded may have fallen short of my aspirations, but nonetheless, I can derive some satisfaction from the accomplishment.

I may not be a better runner than I was a year ago, but my general fitness levels have improved, almost imperceptibly at times, and I have reminded myself of the satisfaction – and frustration – that putting one foot in front of the other can bring.

Then, of course, I had the great pleasure of the company and encouragement of my family as well as good friends, who are all busy in their own right but found time to help me in various ways, by joining me for races, or by offering welcome words of encouragement when I doubted the wisdom of what I was doing. Their support helped me banish reservations and reignite my enthusiasm during bouts of uncertainty.

The runs are completed, my account of the experience is written, my passport is tucked away in the drawer for now, and my case of wine is complete. It's time to undo the laces on my trainers, put my feet up and enjoy a glass of something delicious while I reminisce.

Now, where did I put the corkscrew?

RACES

Switzerland
https://www.genuss-marathon.ch/fr/home.html

Slovenia
https://obalatrail.si/en/

Italy
https://www.prosecco.run/

England
https://www.parkrun.org.uk/molevalley/

Germany
https://www.parkrun.com.de/neckaruferesslingen/

Spain
https://www.sherrymaraton.com/

Slovakia
https://www.kosicemarathon.com/propozicie-khm/

Portugal
http://www.runningwonders.com/meiamaratonadourovinhateiro/

France
http://www.marathon-alsace.com/courses/course-10-kms-vignoble.htm

Hungary
https://futas.maratonman.hu/generali-night-run-2022/

Belgium
http://www.archathle.eu/index.php/nos-organisations/descente-de-la-lesse

Austria
https://www.wachaumarathon.com/

WINE

Switzerland
Bonvin Fendant Sans Culotte 2020

Slovenia
Zaro Malvazija Pivol 2020

Italy
La Tordera, Brunei DOCG 2020

England
Surrey Gold

Germany
Kessler Hochgewächs

Spain
Harveys Amontillado Jerez

Slovakia
Matyšák Prestige Gold Frankovka modrá 2017

Portugal
Aneto Reserva Tinto 2018

France
Domaine Pierre and Frédéric Becht Riesling Christine 2015

Hungary
Szentesi Winery, Kékfrankos 2019

Belgium
Château Bon Baron Acolon 2017

Austria
Edition Chremisa Grüner Veltliner 2021 from Winzer Krems

NEWSPAPERS

Switzerland – *Le Nouvelliste*
Slovenia – *Primorske Novice*
Italy – *Il Gazzettino*
England – *Dorking and Leatherhead Advertiser*
Germany – *Esslinger Zeitung*
Spain – *Diario de Jerez*
Slovakia – *Nový Čas*
Portugal – *Nascer Do Sol*
France – *Dernières Nouvelles d'Alsace*
Hungary – *Magyar Nemzet*
Belgium – *Le Soir*
Austria – *Die Niederösterreichischen Nachrichten*

TUNES OF THE DAY

Switzerland
'Running Up That Hill' – Kate Bush

Slovenia
'The Tide is High' – Blondie

Italy
'Slip Slidin' Away' – Paul Simon

England
'Country House' – Blur

Germany
'Cold as Ice' – Foreigner

Spain
'Sherry Baby' – Frankie Valli

Slovakia
'Pipes of Peace' – Paul McCartney

Portugal
'Into the Valley' – The Skids

France
'Games Without Frontiers' – Peter Gabriel

Hungary
'Dancing in the Dark' – Bruce Springsteen

Belgium

'Rolling on the River' – Tina Turner

Austria

'Keep on Running' – The Spencer Davis Group

POLARIS
PUBLISHING